JANET MELROSE &
SHERYL NORMANDEAU

The Houseplanter

Your Go-To Growing Journal

TOUCHWOOD

TouchWood Editions
touchwoodeditions.com

The information in this book is true and complete to the best of the authors' knowledge. All recommendations are made without guarantee on the part of the authors or the publisher.

Copy edited by Paula Marchese

Proofread by Meg Yamamoto

Cover design, illustrations, and interior illustrations by Tree Abraham

Interior design by Sydney Barnes

CATALOGUING DATA AVAILABLE FROM LIBRARY AND ARCHIVES CANADA

ISBN 9781771514590 (print)

ISBN 9781771514651 (electronic)

TouchWood Editions acknowledges that the land on which we live and work is within the traditional territories of the Lkwungen (Esquimalt and Songhees), Malahat, Pacheedaht, Scia'new, T'sou-ke, and W̱SÁNEĆ (Pauquachin, Tsartlip, Tsawout, and Tseycum) peoples.

We acknowledge the financial support of the Government of Canada through the Canada Book Fund, and the province of British Columbia through the Book Publishing Tax Credit.

Canada BRITISH COLUMBIA

This book was produced using FSC®-certified, acid-free papers, processed chlorine free, and printed with soya-based inks.

Printed in China

29 28 27 26 25 1 2 3 4 5

Dedicated to all indoor plant enthusiasts

Introduction

Whether you have been growing houseplants for many years, or you are just starting out with one or two and already eyeballing numbers three, four, and five in the garden centre, you understand why nurturing houseplants is a fulfilling passion for so many people. From African violets to zzs, we *love* our houseplants! If you're like us, you've crammed as many as you think is reasonable into your home (of course, our significant others rarely agree on what exactly constitutes "reasonable," but that doesn't dampen our enthusiasm). No matter if your collection is burgeoning or bulging, keeping a record of your green babies and tracking your houseplant care routines will help you give them their best lives in your space. It's also fascinating to compare species and varieties and note how they perform as they grow and mature.

You have in your hands a book that requires interaction, but you can choose any or all the parts that best suit you. Flip back and forth between sections, pore through the following plant lists we've offered for every space, every condition, and everyone, and peruse page by page to enjoy all the fun facts and advice we've snuck in. We encourage you to record your observations and information about your houseplants in any way you please: doodle in the margins, use fancy pens and colourful markers (plain ones will work just as well!), and slap sticky notes, cute stickers, and reminders into the journal's interior. We've created a resource that you can use over and over again and in many different ways, and we hope you delight in it.

—SHERYL NORMANDEAU & JANET MELROSE

Houseplants that require little care and are forgiving of neglect

(This is the plant list you've been waiting for.)

All these plants require is you remembering to water them every so often! They can handle just about any light situation, and can even go without repotting for a long time.

- Aloe vera (*Aloe vera*) has thick, fleshy, grey-green leaves with serrated edges.
- Cacti (Cactaceae) as a family come in a wide variety of shapes, sizes, and textures. Perhaps the one thing they all have are sharp spines or modified branches.
- Cast iron plant (*Aspidistra elatior*) is the poster child for the hard-to-kill category, with thick lance-shaped leaves that can grow to 2 feet (60 centimetres) long.
- Golden pothos (*Epipremnum aureum*) is a fast-growing trailing vine that loves to climb a moss pole or other support or hang from a basket.
- Hoya (*Hoya* spp.) are vines with simple, oval-shaped, glossy leaves and five-pointed flowers in umbels that give this plant its common name wax plant.
- Lucky bamboo (*Dracaena sanderiana*) is most often sold braided into lovely shapes and is happy being grown in water or soil.
- Monstera (*Monstera deliciosa*) can be a monster of a plant due to the size—it can get up to 15 feet (4.6 metres) tall, with big glossy green leaves that split when mature.
- Peace lily (*Spathiphyllum* spp.) has glossy, lance-shaped, green leaves and flowers with white blooms composed of a spadix and spathe.
- Rubber plant (*Ficus elastica*) is a stout plant featuring broad, often variegated, waxy evergreen leaves that can grow upwards of 13 feet (4 metres) tall depending on the cultivar.

- Snake plant (*Dracaena trifasciata*) has stiff, evergreen, variegated, lance-shaped leaves that can grow up to 4 feet (1.2 metres) tall.
- Spider plant (*Chlorophytum comosum*) has long, variegated, strap-like leaves and is known for the way it produces "pups" at the end of long stolons.
- zz plant (*Zamioculcas zamiifolia*) is unique with its long arching stalks with opposite oval-shaped glossy green leaves.[1]

Fabulous and flowering

Here are some plants that are so much more than just the sum of their leaves.

- Flaming sword (*Vriesea splendens*): We're cheating a bit by putting a bromeliad on this list, but we know you'll forgive us. The structures we think of as flowers for these plants are actually colourful bracts. If you want a plant that will make jaws drop, this is a suitable candidate.
- Gardenia (*Gardenia* spp.): If you're looking for a houseplant with fragrant flowers but are not prepared to go to the lengths required to get jasmine to bloom, try gardenia instead. The glossy, attractive leaves are a bonus. Look for smaller species to use indoors.
- Hoya (*Hoya* spp.): Also known as wax plants, hoyas can be a bit tricky to bring to bloom, but their incredible fragrance, resembling chocolate, vanilla, or citrus, depending on the species and variety, is such a huge payoff! The more light they have, the more likely they will produce flowers.
- Jasmine (*Jasminum* spp.): There are many species of true jasmine and many of them have exceptional white, highly fragrant blooms. Jasmine will flower only if certain conditions are met: they require cooler temperatures and plenty of humidity to set buds, and they need to enter a period of dormancy before bursting into bloom.
- Lipstick plant (*Aeschynanthus lobbianus*): Striking red blooms that look like lipstick tubes are the big draw for this relatively quick-growing trailer, but let's face it: those thick, deep green leaves are pretty gorgeous, too! The foliage will trail up to two feet (sixty centimetres).
- Other popular blooming houseplants include African violets, orchids of all kinds (including the readily available *Phalaenopsis*), geraniums (*Pelargonium*), fuchsias, begonias, and impatiens.[2]

Meat eaters

Insectivorous plants for your home.

- Butterwort (*Pinguicula* spp.): Butterwort is a low-growing, mounding plant with rosettes of buttery-yellow leaves, which become richer in colour if the plant is grown in plenty of sunlight. If you have a fungus gnat problem with your other houseplants, this is the plant for you: the leaves are sticky with an attractive sap, which traps fungus gnats and other small flying insects.
- Cape sundew (*Drosera capensis*): There are more than 200 species in this genus, but Cape sundew is sometimes found in garden centres. Like something out of a horror movie, Cape sundew has mobile "tentacles" that secrete sap, which attracts insects that are flying by. Enveloped by the tentacles, the insects are eventually digested by the plant's special enzymes. What a way to go!
- Pitcher plant (*Sarracenia* spp.): This interestingly shaped plant has deep pitcher-like leaves. The leaves of most species turn red in colour to attract insects. They also have a particular odour that many insects cannot resist; the insects will then fly into the pitcher structures and be trapped inside by the liquid the plant contains.
- Venus flytrap (*Dionaea muscipula*): If you want to get your young children interested in growing houseplants, get them a Venus flytrap. (Your teens will love them, too, even though they'll pretend they don't.) Venus flytraps do not tolerate drought and they like a lot of sun. They also don't need any nutrients during the winter, which works nicely as flies are at a premium at this time. In the winter, they still require a fair amount of sunlight, but you should reduce the amount you water them.[3]

For growers who want a challenge

Here are some tricky but rewarding houseplants to try.

These plants, along with many others, need just the right conditions and care to thrive. But once you figure out what they need, they are super rewarding, as are all the plants that call your house their home!

- Banana (*Musa* spp.) is a terrific plant to have indoors, but can be fussy, needing a full twelve hours of bright direct light each day. Grow lights can be a boon in keeping bananas happy.
- Bird's nest fern (*Asplenium nidus*) requires consistent moisture in the soil and humidity around its leaves. Don't water the centre as they are prone to crown rot.
- Boston fern (*Nephrolepis exaltata*) needs high humidity around its leaves to prevent crispy leaves, along with bright but filtered light. Provide both and it will reward you with lush growth.
- Croton (*Codiaeum variegatum*) doesn't like being moved or having its soil dry out too much. In both instances it will start dropping leaves to let you know it is unhappy but will quickly perk up with some TLC.
- Elephant ear (*Colocasia esculenta*) needs consistent moisture, or its huge leaves will droop and turn yellow. Place it where it captures your attention!
- Fiddle-leaf fig (*Ficus lyrata*) has those wonderful leaves but is a fussy one indeed. Find its sweet spot right away as it hates being moved. Just the right amount of bright, indirect light is what it needs to thrive.
- Inch plant (*Tradescantia zebrina*) needs consistently moist soil and bright light to keep its variegated leaves glowing. They love to grow, so will require pruning to keep them in shape.
- Moth orchid (*Phalaenopsis* spp.) requires just the right light and a lot of patience while the plant regenerates after blooming, but it is so worth it when those new flower stalks start to emerge.

* Prayer plant (*Maranta leuconeura*) wants moderate amounts of indirect light, and consistently moist but not wet soil. Provide both and it will reward you with those wonderfully coloured leaves.
* String of hearts (*Ceropegia woodii*) is a lovely trailing plant of delicate heart-shaped leaves. It requires just the right amount of water, about every ten days when the soil is dry to touch, but do not let it sit in water or leaves will yellow and die.
* Stromanthe (*Stromanthe sanguinea*) is related to the prayer plant but has wonderful green and red leaves. It wants bright, indirect light, moist soil, and high humidity to be at its best.
* Sweetheart hoya (*Hoya kerrii*) with its heart-shaped leaves only needs a little water every so often for it to thrive.
* Zebra plant (*Aphelandra squarrosa*), with its glossy white-veined green leaves, loves having a humidity tray underneath its pot to provide the 60 percent humidity it craves.[4]

Are you good at remembering to water?

Here are some plant selections that like consistently damp soil.

- African violet (*Streptocarpus* sect. *Saintpaulia*) with its fuzzy leaves and beautiful flowers is well known. It should be bottom watered, allowing the soil to wick up moisture, but don't allow it to sit in standing water.
- Boston fern (*Nephrolepis exaltata*) with those lush and dense fronds needs careful watering so it doesn't dry out.
- Lipstick plant (*Aeschynanthus* spp.) has beautiful red or orange tubular flowers on trailing stems. It needs moist soil, but be careful of overwatering.
- Lucky bamboo (*Dracaena sanderiana*) can be grown in both water and potting soil. If you choose to grow it in the former, the water should be changed frequently. They live longer in potting soil, however.
- Maidenhair fern (*Adiantum* spp.) has a unique texture that is wispy, resembling lace or hair, hence its common name. It loves a nice damp environment.
- Peace lily (*Spathiphyllum* spp.) is a natural moisture meter. If you see the leaves drooping, chances are the soil is too dry and it's time to water.
- Prayer plant (*Maranta leuconeura*) adores being pampered with consistently moist soil. It will send up a prayer of thanks!
- Umbrella plant (*Cyperus involucratus* or *C. alternifolius*) with its drooping palmate leaves thrives in damp soil.
- Zebra plant (*Aphelandra squarrosa*) with its lovely green leaves veined with white often has yellow flowers too. Keep the soil moist for this plant to thrive![5]

Happiest with higher humidity

Most of our houseplants prefer a higher humidity than is usually found in our homes. Many adapt well to the drier air, especially in the winter months, but some demand humidity of at least 70 percent for their health and performance. Ones that want 90 percent humidity need to be in a closed terrarium.

Here is a small selection that really needs that humidity to thrive.

- African violet (*Streptocarpus* sect. *Saintpaulia*) loves humidity in the range of 70 to 80 percent. That's hard to get in our indoor spaces, but they aren't fussy about a lower humidity if they can't get it.
- Air plants (*Tillandsia* spp.) are epiphytic and aren't usually in soil at all. They love to be misted as their leaves can absorb the moisture.
- Bromeliads (Bromeliaceae) prefer humidity in the range of 50 to 75 percent, and higher if it's hot inside. Misting them will prevent leaf burn from too much transpiration.
- Ferns (Polypodiopsida) as a group generally enjoy higher humidity, but the thicker the leaf, the more they can handle drier air conditions.
- Fiddle-leaf fig (*Ficus lyrata*) will experience cracked leaves and browning edges if you don't give it the humidity it needs.
- Gardenias (*Gardenia* spp.) demand high humidity for their flower buds to fully develop and bloom.
- Lipstick plant (*Aeschynanthus radicans*) can handle humidity in the order of 50 percent and loves being misted daily if you can.
- Lucky bamboo (*Dracaena sanderiana*) thrives in humidity of 50 to 70 percent but can handle lower levels just fine.
- Nerve plant (*Fittonia albivenis*) basks in 60 to 80 percent humidity. In drier conditions it will experience drooping and browning leaves.

- Orchids (Orchidaceae) will thrive in humidity of up to 70 percent, even the ones that are from desert-like areas. Too low humidity will result in shrivelling leaves and dropping flower buds.
- Parlour palm (*Chamaedorea elegans*) prefers humidity higher than 50 percent. Less will result in browning leaf tips and dieback.
- Philodendron (*Philodendron* spp.) looks for humidity between 60 and 80 percent to avoid leaf burn and dieback.
- Prayer plant (*Maranta leuconeura*) does best with 60 percent humidity or higher. Dry air will cause drooping and browning leaf tips and edges.[6]

Desert desserts: Plants that prefer to be dry all the time

This list pretty much consists of cacti. (Just remember that there are some plants, such as *Schlumbergera* spp., that have the word "cactus" in the common name but are not actually cacti at all. They have different watering requirements than true cacti.)

There are some succulents that also thrive in these conditions. Here are a few interesting cactus and succulent selections that fit the bill.

- California barrel cactus (*Ferocactus cylindraceus*): This beautifully proportioned barrel-shaped cactus has serious spines and beautiful blooms.
- Eastern prickly pear (*Opuntia vulgaris*): You can likely instantly recall prickly pear's recognizable shape, with large pads surrounded by smaller flat "arms." Prickly pear is easy to care for and not very choosy about what it needs to thrive.
- Horn tree (*Crassula ovata* 'Gollum'): Gotta love that cultivar name! You'll have to repot this fast-growing plant repeatedly throughout its young years, and once it matures, it will actually develop a tree-like "trunk."
- Monstrose cactus (*Cereus hildmannianus* 'Monstrose'): These cacti are sometimes described as weird and misshapen like a monster, but we actually think they look more like coral growing in the sea. Whatever you want to compare them to, they are definitely conversation starters! Monstrose cacti grow very quickly so you'll need to keep up with repotting on a regular basis.
- Pencil cactus (*Euphorbia tirucalli*): This plant doesn't have leaves; instead, its modified thin stems perform the functions of leaves (and look very much like them, too). *E. tirucalli* is a glossy dark green, but you can find red-tipped cultivars as well.
- Peruvian old man cactus (*Espostoa lanata*): Tall, hairy, spiny: everything you want in a cactus (or maybe a man—who are we to say?). This is one of the hirsute cacti covered in downy white hair to protect it from scorching sun.[7]

Perfect palms for large spaces

- Areca or butterfly palm (*Dypsis lutescens*): This is a common outdoor plant in some parts of the United States, although it originates in Madagascar. Indoors, it can reach a size of 5 to 8 feet (1.5 to 2.4 metres). The trunk can take on a gold sheen, which complements the large feathery leaves.
- Cascade palm (*Chamaedorea cataractarum*): Instead of featuring a central trunk like most other palms, cascade palms are more shrub-like, with multiple stems that grow from the base. Cascade palms can reach up to 6 feet (1.8 metres) in height.
- Chinese fan palm (*Livistona chinensis*): The distinctive, fan-like shape of the foliage makes this palm a showstopper, as does the fact that it can reach up to 15 feet (4.5 metres) indoors. If you don't have that kind of space, there are dwarf cultivars that may be more suitable.
- Majesty palm (*Ravenea rivularis*): The long arching fronds of this gorgeous palm make it a standout in a large room (you'll need that space as this plant can very majestically grow up to 12 feet or 3.6 metres tall). Don't position this plant too close to a south-facing window where it will get too much direct light and leaf scorch will occur.
- Parlour palm (*Chamaedorea elegans*): The species epithet refers to the beauty of this plant, and it's impossible to argue. The fern-like leaves of this slow-growing, long-lived palm are stunning. Give parlour palm a bit of space, as it can reach a height of 6 feet (1.8 metres).[8]

Fantastic ferns for that rainforest feel

- Bird's nest (*Asplenium nidus*) has fronds that are smooth and lance shaped, and crinkle the more indirect light you provide.
- Blue star (*Phlebodium aureum*) features bluish-grey fronds that when the plant matures are deeply lobed.
- Boston (*Nephrolepis exaltata*) has bushy but feathery foliage. It is a vigorous grower and can be divided each year.
- Button (*Pellaea rotundifolia*) has fronds with multitudes of small, round leaves and a compact size.
- Crocodile (*Microsorum musifolium*) is lovely for its smooth fronds with markings that look like a crocodile's skin.
- Korean rock (*Polystichum tsussimense*) is a small, finely divided fern with each frond laced with black veins.
- Leatherleaf (*Rumohra adiantiformis*) has triangular, glossy, dark green, finely cut fronds that appear leathery.
- Maidenhair (*Adiantum* spp.) is known for its dainty, fan-like foliage, but needs lots of humidity to thrive.
- Rabbit's foot (*Davallia fejeensis*) has fuzzy epiphytic roots that grow over the sides of the pot looking for all the world like rabbit paws.
- Ribbon or pteris (*Pteris cretica*) often has long, narrow fronds with undulating margins, sometimes with broader leaflets at the ends.
- Staghorn or elkhorn (*Platycerium bifurcatum*) is one fern you can mount on a wall, distinguished by its long irregular fronds that resemble deer antlers.[9]

Got a south-facing window?

Here are some houseplants that love direct light.

- Garden or variegated croton (*Codiaeum variegatum*): The *Codiaeum* genus is large, but this particular species has vibrant variegated foliage that will make your jaw drop: the heavily veined leaves are brilliantly blotched with yellow, orange, red, and green. Once you've seen one, you'll never forget it—and you'll likely add it to your must-have list.
- Mother-in-law's tongue (*Dracaena trifasciata*): Strappy tricolour foliage (yellow, light green, and dark green) and a beautiful architectural form make this plant a standout in any room, but the best thing about it is that it needs very little care to keep it looking good.
- Polka dot plant (*Hypoestes phyllostachya*): The adorable spotted pink, green, and cream variegation on the leaves of this compact plant is irresistible. It's a fun plant to give as a gift or add to a basket of mixed houseplants.
- Ponytail palm (*Beaucarnea recurvata*): Easily identifiable due to the way this plant's thin, stringy leaves curve backwards, ponytail palm is a very slow-growing, long-lived plant that can reach a height of 8 feet (2.4 metres) indoors (it just takes forever!). Its bulbous base is a reservoir for water. (And . . . it's not a palm at all, despite its common name!)
- Most cacti and succulents (as you already knew!).[10]

Lacking light?

These plants can handle those low light situations, though will likely not grow much, and grow slowly. Many evolved in the dim light of tropical forests.

- Anthurium (*Anthurium* spp.) can handle low light, but for flowering they prefer brighter, indirect light.
- Arrowhead plant (*Syngonium podophyllum*), with those spade-like leaves in tones of green, white, silver, and pink, can handle low light so long as the plants aren't overwatered.
- Bromeliads (Bromeliaceae) positively thrive in low light conditions and cannot handle any direct light.
- Chinese evergreen (*Aglaonema commutatum*), a member of the arum family, can thrive nicely in low light.
- Corn plant (*Dracaena fragrans*), with those strap-like leaves on long stalks, likes the indirect light of low light conditions.
- Dumb cane (*Dieffenbachia seguine*), another member of the arum family, will tolerate low light levels but grows very slowly.
- English ivy (*Hedera helix*) will enjoy low light levels but beware that variegated varieties may lose their variegation and need to be moved to medium light.
- Peperomia (*Peperomia* spp.), whose foliage comes in a variety of shapes and colours, can adapt nicely to lower light levels, albeit with slower growth.
- Philodendrons (*Philodendron* spp.), some of the easiest plants to grow, tolerate low light levels and growth will be in check.
- Pothos (*Pothos* spp.) enjoy lower, indirect light as direct light scorches their leaves.
- Prayer plant (*Maranta leuconeura*) enjoys a low light situation, and will not lose that wonderful colour and variegation in its leaves.
- zz plant (*Zamioculcas zamiifolia*) is another that takes to a dark corner with enthusiasm, and as a bonus won't get so big it outgrows its pot so fast.[11]

Big, bold, and beautiful

Focal plants for your more spacious areas.

* Banana plant (*Musa acuminata*) grows up to 10 feet (3 metres) tall, with those large fan-shaped leaves.
* Corn plant (*Dracaena fragrans*) comes with thick stalks topped with new growth. It can get to be 12 feet (3.6 metres) but you can keep it at the height you want by slicing off the top of the stalk.
* Croton (*Codiaeum variegatum*) grows slowly but can end up being 8 feet (2.4 metres) tall, with colourful variegated leaves.
* Dragon tree (*Dracaena marginata*) often grows some 8 feet (2.4 metres) tall with long strap-like leaves.
* Dumb cane (*Dieffenbachia seguine*) grows anywhere from 3 feet (1 metre) to upwards of 10 feet (3 metres) tall, with large oval leaves streaked white, cream, or yellow.
* Elephant ear (*Colocasia esculenta*) is known for its huge leaves that come directly from the base of the plant.
* Fiddle-leaf fig (*Ficus lyrata*) can grow 10 feet (3 metres) tall, with big violin-shaped leaves.
* Majesty palm (*Ravenea rivularis*) has majesty in spades, growing up to 10 feet (3 metres) tall with stiff fronds.
* Money tree (*Pachira aquatica*) grows some 6 to 8 feet (1.8 to 2.4 metres) tall, often with braided stems and palmate leaves to add distinction.
* Monstera (*Monstera deliciosa*) easily grows some 15 feet (4.6 metres) if you let it, following its inclination to grow up tree trunks in its natural habitat.
* Norfolk pine (*Araucaria heterophylla*) can grow up to 9 feet (2.7 metres) tall, with unique pine-like needles on long branches.
* Pencil cactus (*Euphorbia tirucalli*), known for its thin, cylindrical branches no wider than the width of a pencil, can grow up to 6 feet (1.8 metres) tall.

* Ponytail palm (*Beaucarnea recurvata*) has a single broad trunk with a mass of strap-like leaves emerging from the top. It can easily grow 6 to 8 feet (1.8 to 2.4 metres) tall and as wide as the pot it is in.
* Rubber tree (*Ficus elastica*) often grows some 10 feet (3 metres) tall indoors, with those big, broad, oval leaves.
* Spineless yucca (*Yucca elephantipes*) is a slow grower, topping out at about 5 feet (1.5 metres) with a thick stalk topped by sword-like leaves.
* Weeping fig (*Ficus benjamina*) has slender branches and drooping glossy leaves. It grows to between 3 and 6 feet (1 to 2 metres) tall at maturity.[12]

Minuscule and marvellous

These are some of the teeny tiny plants you have been looking for.

- Air plants (*Tillandsia* spp.): These fascinating plants don't require any soil to grow and are incredibly easy to care for (if you remember that they need water!). They range from two to twelve inches (five to thirty centimetres) in height.
- Baby's tears (*Soleirolia soleirolii*): This is one of those plants that make you go "awwwww." Baby's tears grow very quickly into a dense mound of adorable bright green round leaves, but it reaches a height of only about four inches (ten centimetres). Don't let this baby dry out between waterings or you'll risk browning and dieback of stems and foliage.
- Dancing lady orchid (*Oncidium* 'Twinkle'): If orchids are your thing, a miniature oncidium is one to add to your collection! The white floral sprays of 'Twinkle' can reach ten inches (twenty-five centimetres) in length, but the plant itself is only six inches (fifteen centimetres) tall. As a bonus, the profuse tiny flowers are fragrant.
- Zebra plant (*Haworthiopsis attenuata*): This distinctively dark green and white striped succulent is commonly found in garden centres. It is a forgiving plant for those who are new to growing succulents as it's difficult to harm, although too much water will definitely do it in. It will grow to about five inches (twelve centimetres) in height.
- If you love African violets, add the micromini (up to three inches or seven centimetres tall) or mini (up to six inches or fifteen centimetres) cultivars to your list of tiny plants. There are so many to choose from, including variegated and cream- or white-leaved types, with flowers of all colours.
- Many succulents and cacti come in small packages as well, so seek out some of your diminutive favourites for your space.[13]

Hangers and climbers

If you want your plants to reach for the (metaphorical) sky or to cascade and trail, these are a few that fit the bill.

- Asparagus fern (*Asparagus setaceus*): Those leaves you see on your asparagus fern? They're not leaves at all; they're modified stems called cladodes. (Test that one out at your next botanical trivia night!) Whatever they are, their feathery texture is what makes asparagus fern an elegant statement plant. In its native South African habitat, the thin climbing stems can reach up to 8 feet (2.4 metres) in length, but even at its happiest in your house, half that size is expected.
- Golden pothos (*Epipremnum aureum*): There are fifteen different species of pothos and countless cultivars to choose from, but golden pothos is one you'll be able to readily find in most garden centres and plant shops. The variegated gold and green leaves and trailing habit—as well as their minimal needs and rapid growth—make them a popular choice. They can also handle low light, but their colour will be enhanced by sufficient rays.
- Heartleaf philodendron (*Philodendron scandens*): Get out your moss poles! This gorgeous climber with the attractive heart-shaped leaves can reach up to three feet (ninety centimetres) or more, so having something beautiful to give it vertical support is necessary.
- Polynesian ivy (*Elatostema repens* var. *pulchrum*): This trailing beauty, with gorgeous purple and green leaves on two-foot-long (sixty-centimetre) stems, is not quite as low-maintenance as some of the other plants in this book, but if you're up for a challenge, it's worth trying. Offer Polynesian ivy plenty of humidity, don't let the soil dry out completely, and keep it out of cold drafts, and you're on your way to a satisfied houseplant.

- Spider plant (*Chlorophytum comosum* 'Vittatum'): Spider plants may be ubiquitous, but it's just because we can't get enough of this easy-care plant that propagates so readily via cuttings that we always have plenty to share with friends and family (and, just for fun, the plantlets are adorably nicknamed spiderettes). 'Vittatum' is a familiar cultivar, with strappy green leaves that have a stripe of cream down the middle. The elegant arching growth habit is ideal for baskets.
- String of turtles (*Peperomia prostrata*): The species epithet means "to throw oneself to the ground," so you can imagine the growth habit of this pretty jewel: low-growing and creeping. The leaves (which have an oval shape that resembles the shells of turtles) are abundant and attractive as they spill out of pretty containers on long stems.[14]

Colourful candidates

Foliage plants that wow!

We've already mentioned the unique and vibrantly coloured garden croton and polka dot plant (page 20), but there are many other colourful foliage plants that will stop you in your tracks at the garden centre and make you haul out your credit card. Here are a few.

- Chinese evergreen 'Hot Pink Valentine Wishes' (*Aglaonema* 'Hot Pink Valentine Wishes'): This must-have plant features brilliant green and pink leaves. Young plants are compact and tidy, but Chinese evergreen tends to open its form a bit as it matures.
- Coleus (*Plectranthus scutellarioides*): Often considered a garden annual (and for good reason, as they work beautifully in beds and containers), coleus make fantastic houseplants, too! With their bold, bright, and unusual foliage shapes, they tantalize the houseplant collector in us all. One of the more fascinating series of coleus selections is 'Under the Sea', developed by researchers at the University of Saskatchewan.
- Nerve plant (*Fittonia* spp.): Nerve plants have an attractive, dense, and compact growth habit. You'll most commonly find *F. albivenis* (white-veined) nerve plants in garden centres, but if you want brilliant colour, seek out 'Red Star', with deep red veins on green leaves, and 'Pearcei', another red-veined type.
- Painted-leaf begonia (*Begonia rex*): King of begonias, indeed! The variegation of the leaves, often in silvery hues fringed with nearly black veins and margins, makes rex begonias a shoo-in to add to mixed containers for big impact.
- Prayer plant (*Calathea* spp.): Generally available in most garden centres, several varieties of prayer plant have boldly striped or spotted leaves in mosaics of dark and light green, red, purple, and white.[15]

Pretty poison

These houseplants are toxic to humans and pets.

All plants need to be treated with respect. They all contain chemicals used for their natural defences that, if abused, can cause harm if ingested or touched. However, some are more potent and thus toxic to us and our pets, and demand that we take steps to keep ourselves and loved ones from harm.

Here is a selection of the ones to take notice of.

- Aloe vera (*Aloe vera*) is toxic to cats in particular if chewed. The sap is meant for external use only, and not good for dogs and people either, if ingested.
- Bird of paradise (*Strelitzia reginae* and *Caesalpinia gilliesii*) is moderately toxic to people and pets, possibly because it contains hydrocyanic acid.
- Dumb cane (*Dieffenbachia seguine*) is a species in the Araceae family and contains crystals in the sap that if ingested will cause you to temporarily lose your speech due to your swollen tongue and constricted throat. You really have to eat a lot, though, but be safe and keep it out of reach.
- Elephant ear (*Caladium* spp.) contains calcium oxalates that cause the mouth and tongue to swell, and cause vomiting in pets. Guess what? It is in the Araceae family too.
- English ivy and all ivies (*Hedera* spp.) can cause skin irritations, burning throats, rashes, and fevers if eaten in large quantities.
- Jade plants (*Crassula* spp.) are highly toxic to cats and dogs.
- Oleander (*Nerium oleander*) is a gorgeous plant, but extremely dangerous. Don't even have it in the house if children and pets live there or even visit, for that matter!
- Peace lily (*Spathiphyllum* spp.) is really only dangerous if you eat a lot of the leaves. Nevertheless, keep it on a shelf away from children and pets.

- Philodendron (*Philodendron* spp.) is also in Araceae and has similar effects as dumb cane.
- Pothos (*Pothos* spp.) is a close relative of philodendron and causes the same symptoms if ingested.
- Sago palm (*Cycas revoluta*) contains toxins in all parts of the plant. Wear gloves when handling as it can cause vomiting and diarrhea if ingested. Not that you would be so brave or foolhardy as to munch those stiff fronds!
- zz plant (*Zamioculcas zamiifolia*) requires that you handle it with care, especially when dividing it, as you often need to do. Being in Araceae, the leaves are toxic if ingested.[16]

Superstar succulents

So many succulents, so little space! Here is a selection of the most popular and easy to find.

- Air plants (*Tillandsia* spp.) are small epiphytic succulents with many different forms, all of which get their water and nutrients from the air.
- Aloe vera (*Aloe vera*) has long, slender, grey-green leaves on a short stem.
- Black rose aeonium (*Aeonium arboreum* 'Zwartkopf') has large rosettes of red-black leaves atop long stems.
- Burro's tail (*Sedum morganianum*) has long trailing stems with grey-green leaves drooping down from the stems.
- Crown of thorns (*Euphorbia milii*) is a thorny shrub, with thick bright green leaves, that flowers in red, white, or pink throughout the year.
- Hens and chicks (*Sempervivum tectorum*) is often grown outside as a hardy perennial. With its flattened rosettes with sharply pointed leaves, the mother will often grow pups known as chicks.
- Hens and chicks (*Echeveria elegans*) has the same common name and growth pattern as *Sempervivum tectorum* but has rounded leaves and its flower stalk arches with bell-shaped flowers drooping from it.
- Holiday cactus (*Schlumbergera* spp.) is not a cactus at all, but rather a succulent with jointed stems, with buds of flowers emerging from the terminal joint that often coincide with various holidays.
- Jade plant (*Crassula ovata*) is iconic, with its glossy, thick, fleshy leaves on short, stocky stems that thicken and become branch-like over time.
- Living stones (*Lithops* spp.) are a curiosity composed of two succulent leaves that are fused together, with a cleft in the middle, looking for all the world like small stepping stones.

* Ox tongue (*Gasteria* spp.) has rough tongue-shaped leaves variously textured, coloured, and shaped, all emerging from a short stem. A slow-growing plant, it keeps its shape for years.
* Panda plant (*Kalanchoe tomentosa*) is a kalanchoe with a difference, with its fuzzy, grey-green leaves covered in rust-coloured spots.
* String of pearls (*Curio rowleyanus*) is unique in that it forms long stems or strings with pea-shaped leaves, looking for all the world like a rope of pearls.
* Zebra plant (*Haworthiopsis attenuata*) is a slow-growing rosette, known for its striking leaves striped white and green.[17]

Cute and quirky cacti

Just a few of the many cacti that are out there for you to love!

- Barrel cactus (*Ferocactus* spp.) has a barrel-shaped form and is covered by long, rigid spines that truly look ferocious!
- Bishop's cap (*Astrophytum ornatum*), also known as the star cactus, consists of deeply ridged spheres covered with stiff spikes or spines. It often has a silvery sheen to it.
- Bunny ears (*Opuntia microdasys* var. *albispina*) is also called angel's wings for the way new stems grow, two per stem, accented by yellow clusters of hairs all over.
- Feather cactus (*Mammillaria plumosa*) is small sized and its sharp spines are covered up by soft feathery plumes.
- Moon cactus (*Gymnocalycium mihanovichii*) is actually two cacti grafted together, with the green stem of one species on the bottom and the top species being the flower.
- Old man of the mountain (*Oreocereus celsianus*) grows up to a foot (thirty centimetres) and is covered with wispy hairs that protect it against the cold.
- Rat-tail cactus (*Aporocactus flagelliformis*) is a fast-growing cactus with thin stems that can grow up to three feet (one metre) long and love to dangle over the sides of a pot.
- Ric rac cactus (*Disocactus anguliger*) is also called fishbone cactus for its unique form that looks like fishbones. The stems aren't spiny and, as they grow longer, will droop, making this a great one for a hanging basket.
- Saguaro cactus (*Carnegiea gigantea*) has the typical form when we think of a cactus growing in the desert—a straight stem with arms growing out on either side![18]

My Plants

1

MY PLANTS

Plant name (common)

Plant name (botanical)

Cultivar name

Date obtained

Where obtained	*Price*

Foliage colour

Foliage shape

Flowering? Dates:

Colour of flowers?	*Fragrant?*

Growth habit

Outstanding qualities

MY PLANTS

Plant name (common)

Plant name (botanical)

Cultivar name

Date obtained

Where obtained *Price*

Foliage colour

Foliage shape

Flowering? Dates:

Colour of flowers? *Fragrant?*

Growth habit

Outstanding qualities

MY PLANTS

Plant name (common)	
Plant name (botanical)	
Cultivar name	
Date obtained	
Where obtained	*Price*
Foliage colour	
Foliage shape	
Flowering? Dates:	
Colour of flowers?	*Fragrant?*
Growth habit	
Outstanding qualities	

MY PLANTS

Plant name (common)

Plant name (botanical)

Cultivar name

Date obtained

Where obtained *Price*

Foliage colour

Foliage shape

Flowering? Dates:

Colour of flowers? *Fragrant?*

Growth habit

Outstanding qualities

MY PLANTS

Plant name (common)

Plant name (botanical)

Cultivar name

Date obtained

Where obtained	*Price*

Foliage colour

Foliage shape

Flowering? Dates:

Colour of flowers?	*Fragrant?*

Growth habit

Outstanding qualities

MY PLANTS

Plant name (common)

Plant name (botanical)

Cultivar name

Date obtained

Where obtained *Price*

Foliage colour

Foliage shape

Flowering? Dates:

Colour of flowers? *Fragrant?*

Growth habit

Outstanding qualities

MY PLANTS

Plant name (common)	
Plant name (botanical)	
Cultivar name	
Date obtained	
Where obtained	*Price*
Foliage colour	
Foliage shape	
Flowering? Dates:	
Colour of flowers?	*Fragrant?*
Growth habit	
Outstanding qualities	

MY PLANTS

Plant name (common)

Plant name (botanical)

Cultivar name

Date obtained

Where obtained *Price*

Foliage colour

Foliage shape

Flowering? Dates:

Colour of flowers? *Fragrant?*

Growth habit

Outstanding qualities

MY PLANTS

Plant name (common)

Plant name (botanical)

Cultivar name

Date obtained

Where obtained	*Price*

Foliage colour

Foliage shape

Flowering? Dates:

Colour of flowers?	*Fragrant?*

Growth habit

Outstanding qualities

MY PLANTS

Plant name (common)

Plant name (botanical)

Cultivar name

Date obtained

Where obtained *Price*

Foliage colour

Foliage shape

Flowering? Dates:

Colour of flowers? *Fragrant?*

Growth habit

Outstanding qualities

MY PLANTS

Plant name (common)

Plant name (botanical)

Cultivar name

Date obtained

Where obtained *Price*

Foliage colour

Foliage shape

Flowering? Dates:

Colour of flowers? *Fragrant?*

Growth habit

Outstanding qualities

MY PLANTS

Plant name (common)

Plant name (botanical)

Cultivar name

Date obtained

Where obtained *Price*

Foliage colour

Foliage shape

Flowering? Dates:

Colour of flowers? *Fragrant?*

Growth habit

Outstanding qualities

MY PLANTS

Plant name (common)

Plant name (botanical)

Cultivar name

Date obtained

Where obtained	*Price*

Foliage colour

Foliage shape

Flowering? Dates:

Colour of flowers?	*Fragrant?*

Growth habit

Outstanding qualities

Plant name (common)

Plant name (botanical)

Cultivar name

Date obtained

Where obtained *Price*

Foliage colour

Foliage shape

Flowering? Dates:

Colour of flowers? *Fragrant?*

Growth habit

Outstanding qualities

MY PLANTS

Plant name (common)	
Plant name (botanical)	
Cultivar name	
Date obtained	
Where obtained	*Price*
Foliage colour	
Foliage shape	
Flowering? Dates:	
Colour of flowers?	*Fragrant?*
Growth habit	
Outstanding qualities	

MY PLANTS

Plant name (common)

Plant name (botanical)

Cultivar name

Date obtained

Where obtained *Price*

Foliage colour

Foliage shape

Flowering? Dates:

Colour of flowers? *Fragrant?*

Growth habit

Outstanding qualities

MY PLANTS

Plant name (common)

Plant name (botanical)

Cultivar name

Date obtained

Where obtained	*Price*

Foliage colour

Foliage shape

Flowering? Dates:

Colour of flowers?	*Fragrant?*

Growth habit

Outstanding qualities

Plant name (common)

Plant name (botanical)

Cultivar name

Date obtained

Where obtained *Price*

Foliage colour

Foliage shape

Flowering? Dates:

Colour of flowers? *Fragrant?*

Growth habit

Outstanding qualities

MY PLANTS

Plant name (common)

Plant name (botanical)

Cultivar name

Date obtained

Where obtained	*Price*

Foliage colour

Foliage shape

Flowering? Dates:

Colour of flowers?	*Fragrant?*

Growth habit

Outstanding qualities

MY PLANTS

Plant name (common)

Plant name (botanical)

Cultivar name

Date obtained

Where obtained *Price*

Foliage colour

Foliage shape

Flowering? Dates:

Colour of flowers? *Fragrant?*

Growth habit

Outstanding qualities

MY PLANTS

Plant name (common)	
Plant name (botanical)	
Cultivar name	
Date obtained	
Where obtained	*Price*
Foliage colour	
Foliage shape	
Flowering? Dates:	
Colour of flowers?	*Fragrant?*
Growth habit	
Outstanding qualities	

MY PLANTS

Plant name (common)

Plant name (botanical)

Cultivar name

Date obtained

Where obtained *Price*

Foliage colour

Foliage shape

Flowering? Dates:

Colour of flowers? *Fragrant?*

Growth habit

Outstanding qualities

MY PLANTS

Plant name (common)

Plant name (botanical)

Cultivar name

Date obtained

Where obtained	*Price*

Foliage colour

Foliage shape

Flowering? Dates:

Colour of flowers?	*Fragrant?*

Growth habit

Outstanding qualities

MY PLANTS

Plant name (common)

Plant name (botanical)

Cultivar name

Date obtained

Where obtained *Price*

Foliage colour

Foliage shape

Flowering? Dates:

Colour of flowers? *Fragrant?*

Growth habit

Outstanding qualities

MY PLANTS

Plant name (common)

Plant name (botanical)

Cultivar name

Date obtained

Where obtained *Price*

Foliage colour

Foliage shape

Flowering? Dates:

Colour of flowers? *Fragrant?*

Growth habit

Outstanding qualities

Plant name (common)

Plant name (botanical)

Cultivar name

Date obtained

Where obtained *Price*

Foliage colour

Foliage shape

Flowering? Dates:

Colour of flowers? *Fragrant?*

Growth habit

Outstanding qualities

MY PLANTS

Plant name (common)

Plant name (botanical)

Cultivar name

Date obtained

Where obtained	*Price*

Foliage colour

Foliage shape

Flowering? Dates:

Colour of flowers?	*Fragrant?*

Growth habit

Outstanding qualities

MY PLANTS

Plant name (common)

Plant name (botanical)

Cultivar name

Date obtained

Where obtained *Price*

Foliage colour

Foliage shape

Flowering? Dates:

Colour of flowers? *Fragrant?*

Growth habit

Outstanding qualities

MY PLANTS

Plant name (common)

Plant name (botanical)

Cultivar name

Date obtained

Where obtained *Price*

Foliage colour

Foliage shape

Flowering? Dates:

Colour of flowers? *Fragrant?*

Growth habit

Outstanding qualities

MY PLANTS

Plant name (common)

Plant name (botanical)

Cultivar name

Date obtained

Where obtained *Price*

Foliage colour

Foliage shape

Flowering? Dates:

Colour of flowers? *Fragrant?*

Growth habit

Outstanding qualities

MY PLANTS

Plant name (common)

Plant name (botanical)

Cultivar name

Date obtained

Where obtained	*Price*

Foliage colour

Foliage shape

Flowering? Dates:

Colour of flowers?	*Fragrant?*

Growth habit

Outstanding qualities

MY PLANTS

Plant name (common)

Plant name (botanical)

Cultivar name

Date obtained

Where obtained *Price*

Foliage colour

Foliage shape

Flowering? Dates:

Colour of flowers? *Fragrant?*

Growth habit

Outstanding qualities

MY PLANTS

Plant name (common)

Plant name (botanical)

Cultivar name

Date obtained

Where obtained	*Price*

Foliage colour

Foliage shape

Flowering? Dates:

Colour of flowers?	*Fragrant?*

Growth habit

Outstanding qualities

MY PLANTS

Plant name (common)

Plant name (botanical)

Cultivar name

Date obtained

Where obtained *Price*

Foliage colour

Foliage shape

Flowering? Dates:

Colour of flowers? *Fragrant?*

Growth habit

Outstanding qualities

MY PLANTS

Plant name (common)

Plant name (botanical)

Cultivar name

Date obtained

Where obtained	*Price*

Foliage colour

Foliage shape

Flowering? Dates:

Colour of flowers?	*Fragrant?*

Growth habit

Outstanding qualities

MY PLANTS

Plant name (common)

Plant name (botanical)

Cultivar name

Date obtained

Where obtained *Price*

Foliage colour

Foliage shape

Flowering? Dates:

Colour of flowers? *Fragrant?*

Growth habit

Outstanding qualities

A Drop to Drink

Fulfill the watering needs of your houseplants by keeping track of how much water they need and how often you must provide it. If you want, instead of listing individual plants, you can group families together and keep track of exceptions.

2

WATERING

Type of plant

Temperature in the room

Is the plant near a window?

When do I need to water in spring and summer?

How often should I water in fall and winter?

Does the soil need to dry out between waterings?

How much water should I offer?

DATES WATERED (MM/DD)

Houseplant first aid:
Reviving a dehydrated plant

If your plant has wilted due to a lack of water and it seems almost too far gone, attempt one last resuscitation. The top of the growing medium will have crusted over, so use your fingers to gently loosen it. Place the pot in a sink containing tepid water and let the water wick up through the base for an hour. Pull the plant out and allow it to drain. Hopefully, all will be well thereafter!

WATERING

Type of plant

Temperature in the room

Is the plant near a window?

When do I need to water in spring and summer?

How often should I water in fall and winter?

Does the soil need to dry out between waterings?

How much water should I offer?

DATES WATERED (MM/DD)

They're so unusual: Hindu rope hoya

Hindu rope hoya (*Hoya compacta* or *H. carnosa* 'Compacta') is a rather strange mutation of the usual wax plant. It has thick stems with contorted waxy leaves that are curled, twisted, and turned, and that are so heavy the stems dangle over the sides of the container like old ropes. The flowers are pale pink with red centres and, unusually for hoya, are unscented.[19]

WATERING

Type of plant

Temperature in the room

Is the plant near a window?

When do I need to water in spring and summer?

How often should I water in fall and winter?

Does the soil need to dry out between waterings?

How much water should I offer?

DATES WATERED (MM/DD)

Plants tell the seasons through day length, with their leaves being sensitive to how much sunlight they receive, prompting flowering and seed setting.

WATERING

Type of plant

Temperature in the room

Is the plant near a window?

When do I need to water in spring and summer?

How often should I water in fall and winter?

Does the soil need to dry out between waterings?

How much water should I offer?

DATES WATERED (MM/DD)

Dracaena means "female dragon" from the ancient Greek *drakaina* for its resin, which was supposed to resemble dragon's blood.[20]

WATERING

Type of plant

Temperature in the room

Is the plant near a window?

When do I need to water in spring and summer?

How often should I water in fall and winter?

Does the soil need to dry out between waterings?

How much water should I offer?

DATES WATERED (MM/DD)

Banana (*Musa* spp.) is classified as a flowering herb, and the largest one at that!

WATERING

Type of plant

Temperature in the room

Is the plant near a window?

When do I need to water in spring and summer?

How often should I water in fall and winter?

Does the soil need to dry out between waterings?

How much water should I offer?

DATES WATERED (MM/DD)

Orchids can live for up to one hundred years.

WATERING

Type of plant

Temperature in the room

Is the plant near a window?

When do I need to water in spring and summer?

How often should I water in fall and winter?

Does the soil need to dry out between waterings?

How much water should I offer?

DATES WATERED (MM/DD)

In Greek and Roman mythology ivy is associated with eternal life.

WATERING

Type of plant

Temperature in the room

Is the plant near a window?

When do I need to water in spring and summer?

How often should I water in fall and winter?

Does the soil need to dry out between waterings?

How much water should I offer?

DATES WATERED (MM/DD)

Growing plants in pots dates to ancient times, but took off indoors only in the mid-seventeenth century with the invention of glasshouses and conservatories.[21]

WATERING

Type of plant

Temperature in the room

Is the plant near a window?

When do I need to water in spring and summer?

How often should I water in fall and winter?

Does the soil need to dry out between waterings?

How much water should I offer?

DATES WATERED (MM/DD)

Inch plant (*Tradescantia zebrina*) gets its name from its ability to grow an inch a week, even under less-than-ideal conditions.

Kokedama: What is it?

Kokedama, "moss ball" in Japanese, is akin to bonsai. It is a ball of soil that is wrapped with moss and bound together with thin, translucent, filament-like fishing line.

To make a kokedama:

- Take a small plant such as a fern or succulent and wrap the roots with damp sphagnum moss and bind it with fishing line or twine.
- Form a ball with a seven-to-three ratio of moistened peat and bonsai soil that holds together by itself.
- Slice the ball in half and place the roots of the plant between the two halves.
- Then bind the ball with fishing line till all is secure.
- Next, cover the ball with dampened sheet moss and bind it securely with the line or decorative twine.
- Hang in a window or place on a saucer to display.
- To water, soak the kokedama in lukewarm water for about ten minutes, remove and allow excess water to drip out, then rehang or place in a container.

A kokedama will last two to three years with proper care. When the plant is literally growing out of the moss ball, then it is time to replant and start your kokedama off again with a new plant.[22]

WATERING

Type of plant

Temperature in the room

Is the plant near a window?

When do I need to water in spring and summer?

How often should I water in fall and winter?

Does the soil need to dry out between waterings?

How much water should I offer?

DATES WATERED (MM/DD)

Some cacti can go up to two years without water.

WATERING

Type of plant

Temperature in the room

Is the plant near a window?

When do I need to water in spring and summer?

How often should I water in fall and winter?

Does the soil need to dry out between waterings?

How much water should I offer?

DATES WATERED (MM/DD)

A natural latex can be extracted from hoya leaves.

WATERING

Type of plant

Temperature in the room

Is the plant near a window?

When do I need to water in spring and summer?

How often should I water in fall and winter?

Does the soil need to dry out between waterings?

How much water should I offer?

DATES WATERED (MM/DD)

African violets aren't really violets. They just resemble them with their lovely violet-like flowers!

WATERING

Type of plant

Temperature in the room

Is the plant near a window?

When do I need to water in spring and summer?

How often should I water in fall and winter?

Does the soil need to dry out between waterings?

How much water should I offer?

DATES WATERED (MM/DD)

They're so unusual: Pickle plant (*Delosperma echinatum*)

This compact (up to eighteen inches or forty-five centimetres tall) succulent is a favourite among houseplant growers due to its irresistibly cute appearance: the leaves look like tiny spiny pickles! As a bonus, the spines are soft to the touch.[23]

WATERING

Type of plant

Temperature in the room

Is the plant near a window?

When do I need to water in spring and summer?

How often should I water in fall and winter?

Does the soil need to dry out between waterings?

How much water should I offer?

DATES WATERED (MM/DD)

Aloe means "shiny and bitter substance" in Arabic. Don't ingest the sap of this plant, though it is marvellous for external applications.[24]

Which plants die after flowering?

Plants that flower and then die are called monocarpic, meaning "one flower." The hormonal changes that occur as a plant sets a flower, and in some cases seeds and fruit, also lead to senescence. The mother plant literally is giving its all for the next generation.

As houseplants these plants rarely flower, but when they do it can be spectacular. Plants that are monocarpic include:

- *Aeonium* spp.
- Agave—some species
- Arums (Araceae)—some species
- Bromeliads—some species
- Flapjacks (*Kalanchoe luciae*)
- Hens and chicks (*Sempervivum* spp.)
- Palms (Arecaceae)—some species
- *Peperomia* spp.[25]

WATERING

Type of plant

Temperature in the room

Is the plant near a window?

When do I need to water in spring and summer?

How often should I water in fall and winter?

Does the soil need to dry out between waterings?

How much water should I offer?

DATES WATERED (MM/DD)

Ferns first appeared more than 360 million years ago and are one of the oldest types of plants. They propagate by spores rather than seeds.[26]

WATERING

Type of plant

Temperature in the room

Is the plant near a window?

When do I need to water in spring and summer?

How often should I water in fall and winter?

Does the soil need to dry out between waterings?

How much water should I offer?

DATES WATERED (MM/DD)

The oldest houseplant is over 240 years old and lives at Kew Gardens in London, England. It is an Eastern Cape giant cycad (*Encephalartos altensteinii*).[27]

WATERING

Type of plant

Temperature in the room

Is the plant near a window?

When do I need to water in spring and summer?

How often should I water in fall and winter?

Does the soil need to dry out between waterings?

How much water should I offer?

DATES WATERED (MM/DD)

Epiphytic means "on top of plant," as these plants grow on top of other plants but are not parasitic.[28]

WATERING

Type of plant

Temperature in the room

Is the plant near a window?

When do I need to water in spring and summer?

How often should I water in fall and winter?

Does the soil need to dry out between waterings?

How much water should I offer?

DATES WATERED (MM/DD)

Rubber plant (*Ficus elastica*) isn't the species that produces natural rubber. That one is *Hevea brasiliensis* in the spurge family.

WATERING

Type of plant

Temperature in the room

Is the plant near a window?

When do I need to water in spring and summer?

How often should I water in fall and winter?

Does the soil need to dry out between waterings?

How much water should I offer?

DATES WATERED (MM/DD)

Bromeliads get their nutrients from their leaves. They use their roots just for balance.

WATERING

Type of plant

Temperature in the room

Is the plant near a window?

When do I need to water in spring and summer?

How often should I water in fall and winter?

Does the soil need to dry out between waterings?

How much water should I offer?

DATES WATERED (MM/DD)

Potted plants have been grown since ancient times but became popular in the seventeenth century when Sir Hugh Platt, an Englishman, wrote about the possibilities of growing plants indoors.

WATERING

Type of plant

Temperature in the room

Is the plant near a window?

When do I need to water in spring and summer?

How often should I water in fall and winter?

Does the soil need to dry out between waterings?

How much water should I offer?

DATES WATERED (MM/DD)

They're so unusual: String of pearls (*Curio rowleyanus*)

Looking for all the world like a bunch of green peas in a pot, string of pearls is a fast-growing, short-lived, drought-tolerant houseplant that is a ground cover in its native desert habitat of east Africa. They propagate easily via stem cuttings rooted in soil.[30]

WATERING

Type of plant

Temperature in the room

Is the plant near a window?

When do I need to water in spring and summer?

How often should I water in fall and winter?

Does the soil need to dry out between waterings?

How much water should I offer?

DATES WATERED (MM/DD)

There are three species of genera (*Colocasia, Alocasia, Xanthosoma*) that share the common name elephant ear because their leaves resemble the huge ears of elephants![31]

WATERING

Type of plant

Temperature in the room

Is the plant near a window?

When do I need to water in spring and summer?

How often should I water in fall and winter?

Does the soil need to dry out between waterings?

How much water should I offer?

DATES WATERED (MM/DD)

All cacti are succulents but not all succulents are cacti.

WATERING

Type of plant

Temperature in the room

Is the plant near a window?

When do I need to water in spring and summer?

How often should I water in fall and winter?

Does the soil need to dry out between waterings?

How much water should I offer?

DATES WATERED (MM/DD)

The cast iron plant (*Aspidistra elatior*) is also called the bar room plant for its ability to survive just about anything.

WATERING

Type of plant

Temperature in the room

Is the plant near a window?

When do I need to water in spring and summer?

How often should I water in fall and winter?

Does the soil need to dry out between waterings?

How much water should I offer?

DATES WATERED (MM/DD)

Peace lily gets its common name because its blooms look like the white flags of peace.

Buying plants online: Tips for success

As with everything on the internet, plant shopping online is a case of buyer beware. Ensure the seller you wish to use is reputable. Read online reviews from several different (also reputable) sources. Peruse the website thoroughly. Are there a lot of weird links, a lack of information, or mistakes with grammar or spelling? A company that doesn't care about its website isn't one to buy from. Make sure the site has proper security protocols when it comes to payment. Are you paying in your country's currency? Are you going to be faced with surprises regarding shipping and handling charges? If you think you will be, don't plug in those credit card numbers.

As for the plants themselves, is the site using a stock photo or one of the plant you will actually be purchasing? Does that matter to you? How are the plants shipped? What if it is the dead of winter? How are the plants protected during shipping? How far do they have to travel?

What if the plant arrives deader than a doornail? Will you receive any compensation? All these things matter, so researching your purchases thoroughly before you actually plunk down the money is very important.

WATERING

Type of plant

Temperature in the room

Is the plant near a window?

When do I need to water in spring and summer?

How often should I water in fall and winter?

Does the soil need to dry out between waterings?

How much water should I offer?

DATES WATERED (MM/DD)

Norfolk pine is an ancient species in the Araucariaceae family, native to—you guessed it—Norfolk Island in the South Pacific, and reputedly discovered by Captain Cook.

WATERING

Type of plant

Temperature in the room

Is the plant near a window?

When do I need to water in spring and summer?

How often should I water in fall and winter?

Does the soil need to dry out between waterings?

How much water should I offer?

DATES WATERED (MM/DD)

Most pests ignore succulents and cacti.

WATERING

Type of plant

Temperature in the room

Is the plant near a window?

When do I need to water in spring and summer?

How often should I water in fall and winter?

Does the soil need to dry out between waterings?

How much water should I offer?

DATES WATERED (MM/DD)

Orchids are the largest family of flowering plants on Earth, with over 25,000 species—more than there are species of mammals and birds![32]

WATERING

Type of plant

Temperature in the room

Is the plant near a window?

When do I need to water in spring and summer?

How often should I water in fall and winter?

Does the soil need to dry out between waterings?

How much water should I offer?

DATES WATERED (MM/DD)

Orchid flowers are perfectly symmetrical.

Feeding the Potted Beast

Your houseplants will need to be fertilized on a regular basis; otherwise they'll grow peckish and unpleasant. Ensure you're giving them the nutrients they need, when they need them.

3

FERTILIZING	DATES (MM/DD)		
Type of plant			
Time of year			
Type of fertilizer			
Dilution?			
Amount applied			

FERTILIZING	DATES (MM/DD)		
Type of plant			
Time of year			
Type of fertilizer			
Dilution?			
Amount applied			

FERTILIZING	DATES (MM/DD)		
Type of plant			
Time of year			
Type of fertilizer			
Dilution?			
Amount applied			

Cacti are as old as the dinosaurs, dating from about 110 million years ago!

FERTILIZING	DATES (MM/DD)		
Type of plant			
Time of year			
Type of fertilizer			
Dilution?			
Amount applied			

FERTILIZING	DATES (MM/DD)		
Type of plant			
Time of year			
Type of fertilizer			
Dilution?			
Amount applied			

FERTILIZING	DATES (MM/DD)		
Type of plant			
Time of year			
Type of fertilizer			
Dilution?			
Amount applied			

Plants time the time—sort of. They have a circadian rhythm that tells them when to grow, bloom, and even release scents.

FERTILIZING	DATES (MM/DD)		
Type of plant			
Time of year			
Type of fertilizer			
Dilution?			
Amount applied			

FERTILIZING	DATES (MM/DD)		
Type of plant			
Time of year			
Type of fertilizer			
Dilution?			
Amount applied			

FERTILIZING	DATES (MM/DD)		
Type of plant			
Time of year			
Type of fertilizer			
Dilution?			
Amount applied			

They're so unusual: Living stones (*Lithops* spp.)

If you want to make your kids giggle, tell them the other common name for these diminutive oddities: butt plants. Only about 1 inch (2.5 centimetres) tall, lithops are interesting ground cover succulents from Africa. They are easy to look after, but you need to set them up in well-drained, sandy growing medium for them to thrive.

FERTILIZING	DATES (MM/DD)
Type of plant	
Time of year	
Type of fertilizer	
Dilution?	
Amount applied	

FERTILIZING	DATES (MM/DD)
Type of plant	
Time of year	
Type of fertilizer	
Dilution?	
Amount applied	

FERTILIZING	DATES (MM/DD)
Type of plant	
Time of year	
Type of fertilizer	
Dilution?	
Amount applied	

The prayer plant (*Maranta leuconeura*) folds its leaves up each day as if in prayer. At night the leaves fold down, resembling someone bowing over their hands in prayer.

FERTILIZING	DATES (MM/DD)		
Type of plant			
Time of year			
Type of fertilizer			
Dilution?			
Amount applied			

FERTILIZING	DATES (MM/DD)		
Type of plant			
Time of year			
Type of fertilizer			
Dilution?			
Amount applied			

FERTILIZING	DATES (MM/DD)		
Type of plant			
Time of year			
Type of fertilizer			
Dilution?			
Amount applied			

Be sure to repot your zz plant (and all other plants with rhizomatous roots) before it gets large enough to bust out of its pot, breaking the pot as it does so!

FERTILIZING	DATES (MM/DD)		
Type of plant			
Time of year			
Type of fertilizer			
Dilution?			
Amount applied			

FERTILIZING	DATES (MM/DD)		
Type of plant			
Time of year			
Type of fertilizer			
Dilution?			
Amount applied			

FERTILIZING	DATES (MM/DD)		
Type of plant			
Time of year			
Type of fertilizer			
Dilution?			
Amount applied			

Cactus is named after a spiny plant originating in Sicily that was called *kaktos*.[33]

FERTILIZING	DATES (MM/DD)		
Type of plant			
Time of year			
Type of fertilizer			
Dilution?			
Amount applied			

FERTILIZING	DATES (MM/DD)		
Type of plant			
Time of year			
Type of fertilizer			
Dilution?			
Amount applied			

What's in a name?

Some of the common names of houseplants are descriptive, and some honour a region or a person, but many, at first glance, seem simply baffling. You are likely familiar with *Dracaena* spp., often called mother-in-law's tongue (and if you see the sharp, strappy leaves, you can guess where that not-so-polite common name came from), but why on earth would the same plant also be called viper's bowstring hemp? *Dracaena's* native distribution is in Africa, Madagascar, and Asia, and fibres made from its leaves were traditionally used to make durable strings for bows. Just to make things even more exciting (and to reinforce the need to use botanical names over common ones), *D. trifasciata* and some related species are also called snake plant and St. George's sword.[34]

FERTILIZING	DATES (MM/DD)		
Type of plant			
Time of year			
Type of fertilizer			
Dilution?			
Amount applied			

FERTILIZING	DATES (MM/DD)		
Type of plant			
Time of year			
Type of fertilizer			
Dilution?			
Amount applied			

FERTILIZING	DATES (MM/DD)		
Type of plant			
Time of year			
Type of fertilizer			
Dilution?			
Amount applied			

African violets hate getting their leaves wet. Hard water leaves white spots on them.

Keeping a Clean House(plant)

Performing a few grooming and tidying tasks on a regular basis will help your plants maintain their very best appearance.

4

HOUSEKEEPING

Type of plant

DATES WHEN I LOOKED AFTER:

Spent flowers	*Cleaning leaves*	*Pinching*	*Pruning*

HOUSEKEEPING

Type of plant

DATES WHEN I LOOKED AFTER:

Spent flowers	*Cleaning leaves*	*Pinching*	*Pruning*

Dust your plants! Dust on leaves can slow down or prevent photosynthesis.

HOUSEKEEPING

Type of plant

DATES WHEN I LOOKED AFTER:

Spent flowers	*Cleaning leaves*	*Pinching*	*Pruning*

HOUSEKEEPING

Type of plant

DATES WHEN I LOOKED AFTER:

Spent flowers	*Cleaning leaves*	*Pinching*	*Pruning*

Blushing bromeliad (*Neoregelia carolinae* 'Tricolor') has boldly striped cream-white and green strappy leaves that turn rose-hued near the base as the plant prepares to bloom.[35]

Encourage your kids to grow houseplants!

Children are naturally curious, love to touch, and want to learn by doing. They also take pride in accepting new responsibilities. Growing their own houseplants can have a profound effect on children, from calming them down to getting them interested in the natural world.

To get your children or grandchildren interested in growing houseplants:

- Choose plants that are marvellously tactile. Those with feathery leaves like maidenhair fern, or rubbery ones like rubber plant or hoya, or fuzzy like velvet plant.
- Choose ones that are hard to kill off such as snake plant, hoya, or asparagus fern.
- Get them to name their plants so they have ownership of them as well as the responsibility of caring for them.
- Allow them to water and fertilize their plants, under supervision if very young and by themselves as they get older.
- Involve them in tasks such as repotting the plant annually, or propagating for more plants. Spider plant and Christmas cactus are a breeze to grow babies from.
- Older children will be interested in plants with funny names or ones with distinguishing characteristics such as the prayer plant, which folds its leaves up at night, or the appropriately named fishbone cactus.
- Teach them that all living things have a natural lifespan, and some of their plants may die after a time and that it is not their fault if they do so.

HOUSEKEEPING

Type of plant

DATES WHEN I LOOKED AFTER:

Spent flowers	*Cleaning leaves*	*Pinching*	*Pruning*

HOUSEKEEPING

Type of plant

DATES WHEN I LOOKED AFTER:

Spent flowers	*Cleaning leaves*	*Pinching*	*Pruning*

In another case of common names causing massive confusion, the gorgeously textured split-leaf philodendron isn't a philodendron at all. It's part of the genus *Thaumatophyllum*.

HOUSEKEEPING

Type of plant

DATES WHEN I LOOKED AFTER:

Spent flowers	*Cleaning leaves*	*Pinching*	*Pruning*

HOUSEKEEPING

Type of plant

DATES WHEN I LOOKED AFTER:

Spent flowers	*Cleaning leaves*	*Pinching*	*Pruning*

They're so unusual: Polka dot begonia

Polka dot begonia, also called trout begonia (*Begonia maculata*), is a very unusual begonia indeed. It has spotted, elongated, dark green to olive-green leaves that droop. The spots are pale grey to silver grey. As a bonus the undersides of the leaves are a rich dark orange. Its flowers are a pale pink. A very elegant and interesting begonia![36]

HOUSEKEEPING

Type of plant

DATES WHEN I LOOKED AFTER:

Spent flowers	*Cleaning leaves*	*Pinching*	*Pruning*

HOUSEKEEPING

Type of plant

DATES WHEN I LOOKED AFTER:

Spent flowers	*Cleaning leaves*	*Pinching*	*Pruning*

Cacti perform reverse photosynthesis, collecting CO_2 at night when it is cooler, then, when the light returns, converting the stored CO_2 into energy.[37]

HOUSEKEEPING

Type of plant

DATES WHEN I LOOKED AFTER:

Spent flowers	*Cleaning leaves*	*Pinching*	*Pruning*

HOUSEKEEPING

Type of plant

DATES WHEN I LOOKED AFTER:

Spent flowers	*Cleaning leaves*	*Pinching*	*Pruning*

Euphorbia milii is known as crown of thorns because of the belief that it formed the crown of thorns worn by Jesus Christ. In Thailand it is an auspicious plant as the flowers represent the eight saints of Chinese mythology.

HOUSEKEEPING

Type of plant

DATES WHEN I LOOKED AFTER:

Spent flowers	*Cleaning leaves*	*Pinching*	*Pruning*

HOUSEKEEPING

Type of plant

DATES WHEN I LOOKED AFTER:

Spent flowers	*Cleaning leaves*	*Pinching*	*Pruning*

Indoor plants boost humidity, calming dry itchy skin.

HOUSEKEEPING

Type of plant

DATES WHEN I LOOKED AFTER:

Spent flowers	*Cleaning leaves*	*Pinching*	*Pruning*

HOUSEKEEPING

Type of plant

DATES WHEN I LOOKED AFTER:

Spent flowers	*Cleaning leaves*	*Pinching*	*Pruning*

Sago palm (*Cycas revoluta*) isn't a palm at all! It's a cycad that dates to the time of the dinosaurs.

HOUSEKEEPING

Type of plant

DATES WHEN I LOOKED AFTER:

Spent flowers	*Cleaning leaves*	*Pinching*	*Pruning*

HOUSEKEEPING

Type of plant

DATES WHEN I LOOKED AFTER:

Spent flowers	*Cleaning leaves*	*Pinching*	*Pruning*

Oleander (*Nerium oleander*) is one of the most toxic plants in the world.

HOUSEKEEPING

Type of plant

DATES WHEN I LOOKED AFTER:

Spent flowers	*Cleaning leaves*	*Pinching*	*Pruning*

HOUSEKEEPING

Type of plant

DATES WHEN I LOOKED AFTER:

Spent flowers	*Cleaning leaves*	*Pinching*	*Pruning*

Philodendron (*Philodendron* spp.) produces a sugary liquid that attracts ants to it. In return the ants then protect the plant against pests. A nice example of mutualism.

Model employees: Houseplants at work

Houseplants can add huge visual interest to offices, libraries, retail stores, restaurants, and other workspaces. They are more than simply attractive elements of decor, however; they can also elevate moods and provide a calming influence for employees and visitors alike.

Large office complexes and shopping malls may hire professionals to care for their plants, but in a small store or office, the employees will likely be responsible for their care. There won't likely be a lot of time in the schedule to look after plants at work, so selections must be low maintenance, with minimal watering requirements and very little need to be pruned or fertilized. Match the size of the plant to the space: Are you looking for bold and large statement plants or a few small succulents for a tabletop? What about lighting? Is there enough natural light to allow plants to thrive or should you choose plants that can deal with low-light conditions?

One big recommendation for employees who oversee caring for the plants in their workspace: maintain a regular watering schedule. Keep a record of when the plants are watered and who is doing the deed. Multiple people watering randomly and without communication can quickly lead to plant death through rot.

HOUSEKEEPING

Type of plant

DATES WHEN I LOOKED AFTER:

Spent flowers	*Cleaning leaves*	*Pinching*	*Pruning*

HOUSEKEEPING

Type of plant

DATES WHEN I LOOKED AFTER:

Spent flowers	*Cleaning leaves*	*Pinching*	*Pruning*

There are over 400 species of ivy (*Hedera* spp.).[38]

HOUSEKEEPING

Type of plant

DATES WHEN I LOOKED AFTER:

Spent flowers	*Cleaning leaves*	*Pinching*	*Pruning*

HOUSEKEEPING

Type of plant

DATES WHEN I LOOKED AFTER:

Spent flowers	*Cleaning leaves*	*Pinching*	*Pruning*

Zebra plant (*Aphelandra squarrosa*) gets its common name from the white zebra-like markings on its leaves. Another plant with the same common name, *Haworthiopsis attenuata*, also features the unique striping.

HOUSEKEEPING

Type of plant

DATES WHEN I LOOKED AFTER:

Spent flowers	*Cleaning leaves*	*Pinching*	*Pruning*

HOUSEKEEPING

Type of plant

DATES WHEN I LOOKED AFTER:

Spent flowers	*Cleaning leaves*	*Pinching*	*Pruning*

They're so unusual: Donkey's tail

Donkey's tail, also known as burro's tail (*Sedum morganianum*) is a succulent with rows of blue-green teardrop-shaped leaves on stems that slowly grow up to 4 feet (1.2 metres) long. A great plant for a hanging basket or simply left for the stems to droop over the sides of its container on a shelf.[39]

HOUSEKEEPING

Type of plant

DATES WHEN I LOOKED AFTER:

Spent flowers	*Cleaning leaves*	*Pinching*	*Pruning*

HOUSEKEEPING

Type of plant

DATES WHEN I LOOKED AFTER:

Spent flowers	*Cleaning leaves*	*Pinching*	*Pruning*

Almost all cacti are native to the Americas.

HOUSEKEEPING

Type of plant

DATES WHEN I LOOKED AFTER:

Spent flowers	*Cleaning leaves*	*Pinching*	*Pruning*

Tools to keep your houseplants looking spiffy

Having a set of tools, whether bought specially or improvised from items in the home, will serve you well as you care for your houseplants:

- Small trowels
- Sharp scissors of various sizes and shapes
- Tweezers, both curved and straight
- Small brush
- Air dust blower

Also helpful:

- Small scoops for soil and gravel
- Misting bottle
- Small bottle with a nozzle to apply water and/or fertilizer
- Dusting cloth

HOUSEKEEPING

Type of plant

DATES WHEN I LOOKED AFTER:

Spent flowers	*Cleaning leaves*	*Pinching*	*Pruning*

HOUSEKEEPING

Type of plant

DATES WHEN I LOOKED AFTER:

Spent flowers	*Cleaning leaves*	*Pinching*	*Pruning*

Boston fern got its name in 1894, when a shipment of plants arrived in Boston with a new cultivar on board. It was promptly classified as *Nephrolepis exaltata* 'Bostoniensis'![40]

HOUSEKEEPING

Type of plant

DATES WHEN I LOOKED AFTER:

Spent flowers	*Cleaning leaves*	*Pinching*	*Pruning*

Too much of a good thing? Is it possible to have too many houseplants?

We'd like to report that the answer is no, but we'd be wrong. If you have too many houseplants in a small space, they can increase the humidity levels so much that mould can form. You don't want to be breathing in mould spores. Parting with a few of your green wards will be necessary to restore a healthy balance to your living area.

If you have so many plants that they are struggling to get enough light, reconsider the size of your collection. Leggy, stretched, weak, and yellowing plants are not attractive. If you truly want them to thrive, this is not the way to do it.

If you find you don't have enough time to look after them all, you have too many plants. Likewise, if your bank account is taking a hit because you keep buying more, it's time to take a breather and enjoy the ones you have right now.

HOUSEKEEPING

Type of plant

DATES WHEN I LOOKED AFTER:

Spent flowers	*Cleaning leaves*	*Pinching*	*Pruning*

HOUSEKEEPING

Type of plant

DATES WHEN I LOOKED AFTER:

Spent flowers	*Cleaning leaves*	*Pinching*	*Pruning*

Jade plants are considered feng shui, as they take on different meanings depending on which direction you place them in your home.

Upgrading to New Real Estate

For their best health, most houseplants will require repotting during their time with you. Keep notes about the days the deed was done.

5

REPOTTING

Type of plant

Dates repotted

Type of growing medium

REPOTTING

Type of plant

Dates repotted

Type of growing medium

REPOTTING

Type of plant

Dates repotted

Type of growing medium

String of hearts (*Ceropegia woodii*) is a caudiciform plant, having a swollen basal stem or root for water storage.[41]

REPOTTING

Type of plant

Dates repotted

Type of growing medium

REPOTTING

Type of plant

Dates repotted

Type of growing medium

REPOTTING

Type of plant

Dates repotted

Type of growing medium

Natal lilies (*Clivia* spp.) require a period of dormancy to inspire them to bloom indoors. Hold back the watering during this time and put the plant into an area of your home where the temperatures are cool.

REPOTTING

Type of plant

Dates repotted

Type of growing medium

REPOTTING

Type of plant

Dates repotted

Type of growing medium

REPOTTING

Type of plant

Dates repotted

Type of growing medium

They're so unusual: Mexican shrimp plant

If exposed to sufficient sunlight, Mexican shrimp plant (*Beloperone guttata*) will produce interesting floral structures: the red-pink bracts and the small white flowers resemble common underwater crustaceans.

REPOTTING

Type of plant

Dates repotted

Type of growing medium

REPOTTING

Type of plant

Dates repotted

Type of growing medium

REPOTTING

Type of plant

Dates repotted

Type of growing medium

Some succulents wear a sunscreen called farina (epicuticular wax) that looks like a blue or grey dusty coating. Don't wash it off!

REPOTTING

Type of plant

Dates repotted

Type of growing medium

REPOTTING

Type of plant

Dates repotted

Type of growing medium

REPOTTING

Type of plant

Dates repotted

Type of growing medium

Pencil cactus (*Euphorbia tirucalli*) is not a true cactus at all, but rather a euphorbia, making it a relative of the poinsettia.

REPOTTING

Type of plant

Dates repotted

Type of growing medium

REPOTTING

Type of plant

Dates repotted

Type of growing medium

REPOTTING

Type of plant

Dates repotted

Type of growing medium

Houseleeks (*Sempervivum* spp.) are not related to leeks, the vegetable, in any way. They are rosette-forming succulents.

REPOTTING

Type of plant

Dates repotted

Type of growing medium

REPOTTING

Type of plant

Dates repotted

Type of growing medium

REPOTTING

Type of plant

Dates repotted

Type of growing medium

Being close to plants relaxes your brain, allowing you to be more creative, and boosts memory by as much as 20 percent.[42]

REPOTTING

Type of plant

Dates repotted

Type of growing medium

REPOTTING

Type of plant

Dates repotted

Type of growing medium

REPOTTING

Type of plant

Dates repotted

Type of growing medium

They're so unusual: Brain cactus

Brain cactus (*Mammillaria elongata* 'Cristata') looks for all the world like, well, a brain, albeit a green one. Its sinuous and contorted growth occurs from damage to the tissues when young. At the site of the injury the cells multiply faster than the surrounding tissue, hence the contortions that are produced. Often the plants we buy have been manually manipulated to form the brains we see when we buy them. It's a cute little cactus but beware its spines![43]

REPOTTING

Type of plant

Dates repotted

Type of growing medium

REPOTTING

Type of plant

Dates repotted

Type of growing medium

REPOTTING

Type of plant

Dates repotted

Type of growing medium

Flamingo flower (*Anthurium andraeanum*) gets its name from the bright pink colour and elegance of its spathe (that waxy hood found over the spadix, which holds the flowers themselves).

REPOTTING

Type of plant

Dates repotted

Type of growing medium

REPOTTING

Type of plant

Dates repotted

Type of growing medium

REPOTTING

Type of plant

Dates repotted

Type of growing medium

They're so unusual: Lucky bamboo

Lucky bamboo (*Dracaena sanderiana*), also called Chinese water bamboo, is said to provide prosperity to the owner. It isn't a bamboo at all, but rather a species of *Dracaena*, and can be found braided, twisted, and stacked into weird and wonderful shapes. It can be grown equally well in water alone or in moist rich potting soil.[44]

Making More Plants

Helping your leafy charges perpetuate themselves is one of the most satisfying and rewarding aspects of keeping houseplants. (Just watch out for plants restricted by breeders' patents, which will be labelled in stores.)

6

PROPAGATION

Type of plant

Propagation method (division, cuttings, layering)

Was rooting hormone used?

Date of division/cutting/layering (MM/DD)

Date new plants rooted (MM/DD)

Date new plants are potted up (MM/DD)

PROPAGATION

Type of plant

Propagation method (division, cuttings, layering)

Was rooting hormone used?

Date of division/cutting/layering (MM/DD)

Date new plants rooted (MM/DD)

Date new plants are potted up (MM/DD)

There are more than one hundred varieties of lithops.[45]

PROPAGATION

Type of plant

Propagation method (division, cuttings, layering)

Was rooting hormone used?

Date of division/cutting/layering (MM/DD)

Date new plants rooted (MM/DD)

Date new plants are potted up (MM/DD)

Do houseplants growing in bedrooms remove oxygen from the room at night? What is up with that?

There is an element of truth in this old wives' tale.

When plants photosynthesize during the day they absorb carbon dioxide and release oxygen. In the night the process is reversed, and they use oxygen and release carbon dioxide.

However, plants will produce more oxygen than they use, so a room with plants likely has more oxygen than otherwise. In any case, the amount of oxygen used at night by plants is so small compared with the amount in the room that there is no fear of you being asphyxiated. Nor do you need to remove your houseplants from your bedroom each night.

PS: Plants are the world's largest producer of oxygen. Without plants we wouldn't be around!

PROPAGATION

Type of plant

Propagation method (*division, cuttings, layering*)

Was rooting hormone used?

Date of division/cutting/layering (MM/DD)

Date new plants rooted (MM/DD)

Date new plants are potted up (MM/DD)

PROPAGATION

Type of plant

Propagation method (*division, cuttings, layering*)

Was rooting hormone used?

Date of division/cutting/layering (MM/DD)

Date new plants rooted (MM/DD)

Date new plants are potted up (MM/DD)

The word "succulents" comes from the Latin *sucus*, meaning sap.

PROPAGATION

Type of plant

Propagation method (division, cuttings, layering)

Was rooting hormone used?

Date of division/cutting/layering (MM/DD)

Date new plants rooted (MM/DD)

Date new plants are potted up (MM/DD)

Houseplants and feng shui

Feng shui, meaning "wind" and "water," relates to the concept that human life is connected to and flowing with the environment around us. This philosophy, in Asia called *Tao*, meaning "the way," is the way of nature, and part of practising feng shui can include how we place our plants within our homes.

The five elements of feng shui are wood, earth, fire, metal, and water. The wood element speaks to the green of our plants' foliage. Earth can be represented by the growing mediums we use, such as potting soil, pebbles, stones, and pottery. Fire can be represented by brilliant orange, yellow, and red foliage and flowers. Metal can be decorative containers or art. And water might involve an aquarium or other water feature.

The study of feng shui is complex and in many ways mysterious. Our plants placed strategically and incorporating the five elements can create a positive energy in our homes.[46]

PROPAGATION

Type of plant

Propagation method (*division, cuttings, layering*)

Was rooting hormone used?

Date of division/cutting/layering (MM/DD)

Date new plants rooted (MM/DD)

Date new plants are potted up (MM/DD)

PROPAGATION

Type of plant

Propagation method (*division, cuttings, layering*)

Was rooting hormone used?

Date of division/cutting/layering (MM/DD)

Date new plants rooted (MM/DD)

Date new plants are potted up (MM/DD)

Fittonia is often called the nerve plant, not because it is nervous but because the veining on its leaves resembles nerve networks.

PROPAGATION

Type of plant

Propagation method (*division, cuttings, layering*)

Was rooting hormone used?

Date of division/cutting/layering (MM/DD)

Date new plants rooted (MM/DD)

Date new plants are potted up (MM/DD)

PROPAGATION

Type of plant

Propagation method (*division, cuttings, layering*)

Was rooting hormone used?

Date of division/cutting/layering (MM/DD)

Date new plants rooted (MM/DD)

Date new plants are potted up (MM/DD)

Cactus spines are not thorns. They are modified leaves.

PROPAGATION

Type of plant

Propagation method (division, cuttings, layering)

Was rooting hormone used?

Date of division/cutting/layering (MM/DD)

Date new plants rooted (MM/DD)

Date new plants are potted up (MM/DD)

Helpful tools to use when you are propagating your houseplants

One nice thing about growing houseplants: you don't need a garden shed filled with tools to care for them. A few handy things to have include:

- A pair of very sharp scissors for trimming and cutting (you can buy specialty garden scissors with a short blade for these tasks)
- A small trowel for planting and repotting
- Watering can
- Spray bottle or mister
- Gloves
- Glass jars or bottles so you can root cuttings in water (a fancy propagation station is really nice if you have the money and can actually be a piece of decor in your home)
- Tray for propagating cuttings in soil
- Rooting hormone

PROPAGATION

Type of plant

Propagation method (division, cuttings, layering)

Was rooting hormone used?

Date of division/cutting/layering (MM/DD)

Date new plants rooted (MM/DD)

Date new plants are potted up (MM/DD)

PROPAGATION

Type of plant

Propagation method (division, cuttings, layering)

Was rooting hormone used?

Date of division/cutting/layering (MM/DD)

Date new plants rooted (MM/DD)

Date new plants are potted up (MM/DD)

Did you know that the word *chenille* is used in French to denote a type of fuzzy caterpillar? When you see a chenille plant (*Acalypha hispida*), with its woolly-looking flowers, you'll understand how this plant gets its common name.[47]

PROPAGATION

Type of plant

Propagation method (division, cuttings, layering)

Was rooting hormone used?

Date of division/cutting/layering (MM/DD)

Date new plants rooted (MM/DD)

Date new plants are potted up (MM/DD)

PROPAGATION

Type of plant

Propagation method (division, cuttings, layering)

Was rooting hormone used?

Date of division/cutting/layering (MM/DD)

Date new plants rooted (MM/DD)

Date new plants are potted up (MM/DD)

Croton leaves have been used for centuries to produce natural yellow, orange, and red dyes.

PROPAGATION

Type of plant

Propagation method (division, cuttings, layering)

Was rooting hormone used?

Date of division/cutting/layering (MM/DD)

Date new plants rooted (MM/DD)

Date new plants are potted up (MM/DD)

PROPAGATION

Type of plant

Propagation method (division, cuttings, layering)

Was rooting hormone used?

Date of division/cutting/layering (MM/DD)

Date new plants rooted (MM/DD)

Date new plants are potted up (MM/DD)

The lovely trailing *Plectranthus* is in the mint family, even though its leaves resemble those of coleus.

PROPAGATION

Type of plant

Propagation method (*division, cuttings, layering*)

Was rooting hormone used?

Date of division/cutting/layering (MM/DD)

Date new plants rooted (MM/DD)

Date new plants are potted up (MM/DD)

PROPAGATION

Type of plant

Propagation method (*division, cuttings, layering*)

Was rooting hormone used?

Date of division/cutting/layering (MM/DD)

Date new plants rooted (MM/DD)

Date new plants are potted up (MM/DD)

Dieffenbachia has the common name of dumb cane because its sap can numb the tongue (rendering speechlessness). Don't lick this toxic plant.

PROPAGATION

Type of plant

Propagation method (division, cuttings, layering)

Was rooting hormone used?

Date of division/cutting/layering (MM/DD)

Date new plants rooted (MM/DD)

Date new plants are potted up (MM/DD)

PROPAGATION

Type of plant

Propagation method (division, cuttings, layering)

Was rooting hormone used?

Date of division/cutting/layering (MM/DD)

Date new plants rooted (MM/DD)

Date new plants are potted up (MM/DD)

Cacti are often classified as desert cacti or jungle cacti.

Notes

1. Hinsdale, *Never Put a Cactus in the Bathroom*, 47–49; Staehling, *Happy Houseplants: 30 Lovely Varieties to Brighten Up Your Home*, 84.

2. Domoney, *My Houseplant Saved My Life*, 86–87, 138–39; Sibley, *The Big Book of House Plants*, 228; Toscano and Baker, "How to Get Jasmine to Bloom Indoors," Real Simple (website).

3. Staake, "How to Grow a Carnivorous Sundew Plant," Birds and Blooms (website).

4. Myers, "How to Grow and Care for a Banana Tree," The Spruce (website); Vanzile, "How to Grow and Care for Bird's Nest Ferns," The Spruce (website); Hinsdale, *Never Put a Cactus in the Bathroom*, 96–98, 140–41; Rodino, *How to Houseplant*, 121–23; Longfield Gardens (website), "All about Elephant Ears"; New York Botanical Garden (website), "Prayer Plant (*Maranta leuconeura*)"; Johnstone, "How to Grow and Care for Triostar Stromanthe," The Spruce (website); Mahr, "String of Hearts, *Ceropegia woodii*," Wisconsin Horticulture (website); Dyer and Grant, "*Hoya Kerrii*: Complete Plant Care and Growing," Gardening Know How (website); Vanzile, "How to Grow and Care for Zebra Plant," The Spruce (website).

5. Boeckman, "How to Care for African Violets," *The Old Farmer's Almanac* (website); MasterClass (website), "Lipstick Plant Care: 7 Tips for Growing Lipstick Plants"; Vanzile, "How to Grow and Care for *Schefflera* (Umbrella Plant)," The Spruce (website).

6. Canopy (website), "Are Humidifiers Good for Air Plants?"; Mahr, "Bromeliads," Wisconsin Horticulture (website); Vanzile, "How to Grow and Care for Gardenia," The Spruce (website); Bender, "How to Grow and Care for Nerve Plant," Southern Living (website); Finkle, "Do Orchids Need High Humidity?," New York Botanical Garden (website); Steil, "How Do I Care for a Philodendron?," Iowa State University Extension and Outreach (website).

7. Greenery Unlimited (website), "Pencil Cactus Care."

8. Leon, *Plant*, 59; Vanzile, "How to Grow and Care for Parlor Palm," The Spruce (website); Jones, "How to Grow and Care for a Cat Palm Indoors," The Spruce (website); Vanzile, "How to Grow and Care for Majesty Palm," The Spruce (website).

9. Sears, "How to Grow and Care for Blue Star Fern," The Spruce (website); Di Lallo, "Button Fern Indoor Requirements—How to Grow Button Fern Houseplants," Gardening Know How (website); Perennial Pastimes (website), "Unraveling the Mystery (and History) of the Crocodile Fern"; Peerless, *How Not to Kill Your Houseplant*, 110–11; Carwood, "How to Plant, Grow and Care for Korean Rock Ferns," *Better Homes and Gardens* (website); Missouri Botanical Garden (website),

"*Rumohra adiantiformis*"; Jones, "How to Grow and Care for Maidenhair Fern Indoors," The Spruce (website); Vanzile, "How to Grow and Care for Rabbit's Foot Fern," The Spruce (website); North Carolina State Extension (website), "*Pteris.*"

10. Sibley, *The Big Book of House Plants*, 244; Mikolajski, *Grow Your Own Pet Plants*, 72; Leon, *Plant*, 142.

11. Peerless, *How Not to Kill Your Houseplant*, 40–41; Tilley and Ellis, "Syngonium (Arrowhead Plant): Complete Care and Gardening Guide," Gardening Know How (website); Vanzile, "How to Grow and Care for Chinese Evergreen (*Aglaonema*) Indoors," The Spruce (website); Bradley and McAlpine, "31 Best Low-Light Indoor Plants to Brighten Up Your Home," *Better Homes and Gardens* (website).

12. Hinsdale, *What Is My Plant Telling Me?*, 50–51, 112–13; Peerless, *How Not to Kill Your Houseplant*, 136–37; Vanzile, "How to Grow and Care for Croton Plants," The Spruce (website); Salisbury Greenhouse (website), "How to Care for Dragon Tree"; Gillette, "How to Care for a Fiddle Leaf Fig and Keep It Thriving," The Spruce (website); Sears, "How to Grow and Care for the Money Tree," The Spruce (website); Heath and Aloi, "How to Grow and Care for *Monstera Deliciosa*," The Spruce (website); Boeckmann, "How to Care for Ponytail Palms," *The Old Farmer's Almanac* (website); Vanzile, "How to Grow and Care for Rubber Plant Indoors," The Spruce (website); Vanzile, "How to Grow and Care for Weeping Fig," The Spruce (website).

13. Mikolajski, *Grow Your Own Pet Plants*, 112; Sibley, *The Big Book of House Plants*, 85; McIntosh, "How to Grow and Care for Baby's Tears," The Spruce (website); Smithsonian Gardens (website), "Care of *Oncidium*."

14. Leon, *Plant*, 34, 61, 102.

15. Cooper, "Pink-Leaved Plants for Valentine's Day," Weston Nurseries (website).

16. Kansas Poison Center (website), "Aloe Vera"; Hollinger, "Bird of Paradise Poisoning in Dogs," Wag! (website); Simpson, "Araceae," Science Direct (website); ASPCA (website), "Poisonous Plants."

17. Hassani, "59 Succulents You Should Grow That Are Perfectly Low-Maintenance," The Spruce (website); Vanzile, "How to Grow and Care for *Gasteria*," The Spruce (website); Badgett, "Panda Plant Care—How to Grow a Panda Plant Indoors," Gardening Know How (website).

18. Sansone and Robertson, "30 Different Types of Cactus You Can Grow at Home," Country Living (website); Staehling, *Happy Houseplants: 30 Lovely Varieties to Brighten Up Your Home*, 74; Kilgore, "30 Identification Types of Cacti Chart with Pictures by Location, Species, Size," 8 Billion Trees (website).

19. Houseplant Resource Center (website), "*Hoya Carnosa* 'Compacta' Care Guide—Hindu Rope Plant."

20. Ambius (website), "All about the Dracaena Plant."

21. National Trust (website), "A Potted History of Houseplants."

22. Missouri Botanical Garden (website), "Visual Guides: Kokedama."

23. Gast, "How to Care for the Quirky Pickle Plant," Rural Sprout (website).

24. Surjushe et al. "Aloe Vera: A Short Review," National Library of Medicine.

25. Grant, "Growing Monocarpic Succulents: What Succulents Are Monocarpic," Gardening Know How (website).

26. University of Waterloo: Earth Sciences (website), "Fern Fossils."

27. Avis-Riordan, "Meet the Oldest Pot Plant in the World," Royal Botanic Gardens Kew.

28. Petruzzello, "Epiphyte," Britannica (website).

29. Apple Rubber (website), "How is Natural Rubber Made?"

30. Vanzile, "How to Grow and Care for String of Pearls Plant," The Spruce (website).

31. Mahr, "Elephant Ears (Colocasia, Alocasia, and Xanthosoma)," Wisconsin Horticulture (website).

32. Snakenberg, "Orchids—A Diverse Family of Plants and People," Denver Botanic Gardens (website).

33. Dean, "The Etymology of the Word Artichoke," Bon Appetit (website).

34. Stamen and Stem (website), "Plant Profiles: Sansevieria (Snake Plant)."

35. Plantquility (website), "Blushing Bromeliad Plant Care Guide."

36. Aloi, "How to Grow and Care for *Begonia Maculata*," The Spruce (website).

37. CactusCare, "How Cacti Perform Photosynthesis (in a Different Way)."

38. Brillon, "17 Types of Ivy Plants You Should Know," Epic Gardening (website).

39. Rodino, *How to Houseplant*, 88–89.

40. Mahr, "Boston Fern, *Nephrolepis exaltata* 'Bostoniensis'," Wisconsin Horticulture (website).

41. Staehling, *Happy Houseplants: 30 Lovely Varieties to Brighten Up Your Home*, 86.

42. Bloomscape (website), "How Office Plants Lower Stress and Improve Concentration."

43. Grant, "What Is Brain Cactus: Cristata Information and Care," Gardening Know How (website).

44. Rodino, How to Houseplant, 114–15.

45. Sloan, "Lithops Cultivation," Mediterranean Garden Society (website).

46. Slaymaker, "Bring Good Luck and Positive Vibes with These 17 Feng Shui Plants," Lively Root (website).

47. Mahr, "Chenille Plant, *Acalypha hispida*," Wisconsin Horticulture (website).

Sources

Aloi, Peg. "How to Grow and Care for *Begonia Maculata*." The Spruce (website). Last updated September 2, 2024. thespruce.com/begonia-maculata-care-guide-6743839.

Ambius (website). "All about the Dracaena Plant." Accessed September 1, 2024. ambius.com/resources/blog/plant-profile/the-origins-of-dracaena-plant.

Apple Rubber (website). "How Is Natural Rubber Made?" Accessed September 1, 2024. applerubber.com/blog/how-is-natural-rubber-made/.

ASPCA (website). "Poisonous Plants." Accessed September 1, 2024. aspca.org/pet-care/animal-poison-control/toxic-and-non-toxic-plants.

Avis-Riordan, Katie. "Meet the Oldest Pot Plant in the World." Royal Botanic Gardens Kew. July 23, 2019. kew.org/read-and-watch/oldest-pot-plant-in-world-eastern-cape-giant-cycad.

Badgett, Becca. "Panda Plant Care—How to Grow a Panda Plant Indoors." Gardening Know How (website). Last updated March 11, 2021. gardeningknowhow.com/houseplants/kalanchoe/indoor-panda-plant-care.htm.

Bender, Steve. "How to Grow and Care for Nerve Plant." Southern Living (website). Last updated May 3, 2024. southernliving.com/garden/indoors/nerve-plant.

Bloomscape (website). "How Office Plants Lower Stress and Improve Concentration." Accessed September 1, 2024. bloomscape.com/green-living/office-plants-lower-stress-improve-concentration/.

Boeckman, Catherine. "How to Care for African Violets." *The Old Farmer's Almanac* (website). Last updated July 15, 2024. almanac.com/plant/african-violets.

———. "How to Care for Ponytail Palms." *The Old Farmer's Almanac* (website). Last updated July 2, 2024. almanac.com/plant/ponytail-palms.

Bradley, Nicole, and Lynn McAlpine. "31 Best Low-Light Indoor Plants to Brighten Up Your Home." *Better Homes and Gardens* (website). Last updated January 22, 2024. bhg.com/gardening/houseplants/projects/indoor-plants-for-low-light/.

Brillon, Kaleigh. "17 Types of Ivy Plants You Should Know." Epic Gardening (website). Last updated June 22, 2023. epicgardening.com/types-of-ivy/.

CactusCare. "How Cacti Perform Photosynthesis (in a Different Way)." Accessed September 1, 2024. cactuscare.com/photosynthesis/.

Canopy (website). "Are Humidifiers Good for Air Plants?" Last updated May 2023. getcanopy.co/blogs/news/are-humidifiers-good-for-air-plants.

Carwood, Derek. "How to Plant, Grow and Care for Korean Rock Ferns." *Better*

Homes and Gardens (website). February 3, 2023. bhg.com/how-to-grow-korean-rock-fern-6834456.

Cooper, Catherine. "Pink-Leaved Plants for Valentine's Day." Weston Nurseries (website). Accessed September 1, 2024. westonnurseries.com/pink-leaved-plants-for-valentines-day/.

Dean, Sam. "The Etymology of the Word Artichoke." Bon Appetit (website). May 17, 2019. bonappetit.com/test-kitchen/ingredients/article/the-etymology-of-the-word-artichoke.

Di Lallo, Raffaele. "Button Fern Indoor Requirements—How to Grow Button Fern Houseplants." Gardening Know How (website). February 9, 2023. gardeningknowhow.com/houseplants/ferns-houseplants/button-fern-indoors.htm.

Domoney, David. *My Houseplant Saved My Life*. New York: Dorling Kindersley, 2021.

Dyer, Mary H., and Bonnie L. Grant. "*Hoya Kerrii*: Complete Plant Care and Growing." Gardening Know How (website). Last updated July 16, 2024. gardeningknowhow.com/houseplants/sweetheart-hoya/sweetheart-hoya-plant-care.htm.

Finkle, Anita. "Do Orchids Need High Humidity?" New York Botanical Garden (website). Last updated May 25, 2024. libanswers.nybg.org/faq/222519.

Gast, Mickey. "How to Care for the Quirky Pickle Plant." Rural Sprout (website). December 7, 2022. ruralsprout.com/pickle-plant/.

Gillette, Barbara. "How to Care for a Fiddle Leaf Fig and Keep It Thriving." The Spruce (website). Last updated August 15, 2024. thespruce.com/grow-fiddle-leaf-fig-indoors-1902756.

Grant, Bonnie. "Growing Monocarpic Succulents: What Succulents Are Monocarpic." Gardening Know How (website). Accessed September 1, 2024. gardeningknowhow.com/ornamental/cacti-succulents/scgen/what-are-monocarpic-succulents.htm.

Grant, Bonnie L. "What Is Brain Cactus: Cristata Information and Care." Gardening Know How (website). March 1, 2023. gardeningknowhow.com/ornamental/cacti-succulents/mammillaria/brain-cactus-information.htm.

Greenery Unlimited (website). "Pencil Cactus Care." Accessed September 1, 2024. greeneryunlimited.co/pages/pencil-cactus-care.

Hassani, Nadia. "59 Succulents You Should Grow That Are Perfectly Low-Maintenance." The Spruce (website). Last updated July 9, 2024. thespruce.com/types-of-succulents-7090763.

Heath, Sienna, and Peg Aloi. "How to Grow and Care for *Monstera Deliciosa*." The Spruce (website). Last updated August 15, 2024. thespruce.com/how-to-grow-monstera-deliciosa-5072671.

Hinsdale, Emily L. Hay. *Never Put a Cactus in the Bathroom*. New York: Simon & Schuster, 2021.

———. *What Is My Plant Telling Me?* New York: Simon & Schuster, 2022.

Hollinger, Hannah. "Bird of Paradise Poisoning in Dogs." Wag! (website). Last updated October 29, 2021. wagwalking.com/condition/bird-of-paradise-poisoning.

Houseplant Resource Center (website). "*Hoya Carnosa* Compacta Care Guide—Hindu Rope Plant." Accessed September 1, 2024. houseplantresourcecenter.com/2022/05/hoya-carnosa-compacta-care-guide-hindu-rope-plant/.

Johnstone, Emma. "How to Grow and Care for Triostar Stromanthe." The Spruce (website). Last updated September 10, 2022. thespruce.com/triostar-stromanthe-plant-profile-5069126.

Jones, Alexandra. "How to Grow and Care for Cat Palm Indoors." The Spruce (website). Last updated June 21, 2024. thespruce.com/cat-palm-care-guide-7559170.

———. "How to Grow and Care for Maidenhair Fern Indoors." The Spruce (website). Last updated March 1, 2024. thespruce.com/grow-adiantum-ferns-1902722.

Kansas Poison Center (website). "Aloe Vera." Accessed September 1, 2024. kansaspoisoncenter.com/poisons/plants-and-mushrooms/aloe-vera.

Kilgore, Georgette. "30 Identification Types of Cacti Chart with Pictures by Location, Species, Size." 8 Billion Trees (website). Last updated February 7, 2024. 8billiontrees.com/gardening/identification-types-of-cacti-chart/.

Leon, Gynelle. *Plant*. London: Octopus Publishing Group, 2021.

Longfield Gardens (website). "All About Elephant Ears." Accessed September 1, 2024. longfield-gardens.com/article/all-about-elephant-ears.

Mahr, Susan. "Boston Fern, *Nephrolepis exaltata* 'Bostoniensis'." Wisconsin Horticulture (website). hort.extension.wisc.edu/articles/boston-fern-nephrolepis-exaltata-bostoniensis/.

———. "Bromeliads." Wisconsin Horticulture (website). Accessed September 1, 2024. hort.extension.wisc.edu/articles/bromeliads/.

———. "Chenille Plant, *Acalypha hispida*." Wisconsin Horticulture (website). hort.extension.wisc.edu/articles/chenille-plant-acalypha-hispida/.

———. "Elephant Ears (*Colocasia*, *Alocasia*, and *Xanthosoma*)." Wisconsin Horticulture (website). hort.extension.wisc.edu/articles/elephant-ears-colocasia-alocasia-and-xanthosoma/.

———. "String of Hearts, *Ceropegia woodii*." Wisconsin Horticulture (website). hort.extension.wisc.edu/articles/string-of-hearts-ceropegia-woodii/.

MasterClass (website). "Lipstick Plant Care: 7 Tips for Growing Lipstick Plants." Last updated September 29, 2021. masterclass.com/articles/lipstick-plant-care-guide.

McIntosh, Jamie. "How to Grow and Care for Baby's Tears." The Spruce (website). Last updated February 6, 2024. thespruce.com/baby-tears-plant-4582879.

Mikolajski, Andrew. *Grow Your Own Pet Plants*. France: Smith Street Books, 2019.

Missouri Botanical Garden (website). "*Rumohra adiantiformis*." Accessed September 1, 2024. missouribotanicalgarden.org/PlantFinder/PlantFinderDetails.aspx?taxonid=285696.

———. "Visual Guides: Kokedama." Accessed September 1, 2024. missouribotanicalgarden.org/gardens-gardening/your-garden/help-for-the-home-gardener/advice-tips-resources/visual-guides/how-to-make-a-kokedama.

Myers, Vanessa Richins. "How to Grow and Care for a Banana Tree." The Spruce (website). Last updated August 2, 2024. thespruce.com/banana-tree-growing-profile-3269353.

National Trust (website). "A Potted History of Houseplants." Accessed September 1, 2024. nationaltrust.org.uk/discover/history/gardens-landscapes/a-potted-history-of-houseplants.

New York Botanical Garden (website). "Prayer Plant (*Maranta leuconeura*)." Last updated May 24, 2024. libguides.nybg.org/prayerplant.

North Carolina State Extension (website). "*Pteris*." Accessed September 1, 2024. plants.ces.ncsu.edu/plants/pteris/.

Peerless, Veronica. *How Not to Kill Your Houseplant*. New York: DK Publishing, 2017.

Perennial Pastimes (website). "Unraveling the Mystery (and History) of the Crocodile Fern." Accessed September 1, 2024. perennialpastimes.com/2024/01/14/unraveling-the-mystery-and-history-of-the-crocodile-fern/.

Petruzzello, Melissa. "Epiphyte." Britannica (website). Accessed September 1, 2024. britannica.com/plant/epiphyte.

Plantquility (website). "Blushing Bromeliad Plant Care Guide." Accessed September 1, 2024. plantquility.com/blogs/plant-care-guide/blushing-bromeliad-plant-care-guide.

Rodino, Heather. *How to Houseplant*. New York: Sterling Publishing, 2019.

Salisbury Greenhouse (website). "How to Care for Dragon Tree." Accessed September 1, 2024. salisburygreenhouse.com/how-to-care-for-dragon-tree/.

Sansone, Arrica Elin, and Terri Robertson. "30 Different Types of Cactus You Can Grow at Home." Country Living (website). Last updated June 11, 2024. countryliving.com/gardening/g28365636/types-of-cactus-species/.

Sears, Cori. "How to Grow and Care for Blue Star Fern." The Spruce (website). Last updated April 3, 2024. thespruce.com/blue-star-fern-care-7553051.

———. "How to Grow and Care for the Money Tree." The Spruce (website). Last updated December 19, 2023. thespruce.com/growing-guiana-chestnut -indoors-4773440.

Sibley, Emma. *The Big Book of House Plants*. London: Quadrille, 2023.

Simpson, Michael G. "Araceae." Science Direct (website). 2010. sciencedirect.com /topics/pharmacology-toxicology-and-pharmaceutical-science/araceae.

Slaymaker, Matt. "Bring Good Luck and Positive Vibes with These 17 Feng Shui Plants." Lively Root (website). June 17, 2024. livelyroot.com/blogs/plant-care/feng-shui-plants.

Sloan, Andrew. "Lithops Cultivation." Mediterranean Garden Society (website). April 2020. mediterraneangardensociety.org/100-lithops.html.

Smithsonian Gardens (website). "Care of *Oncidium*." Accessed September 1, 2024. gardens.si.edu/collections/plants/orchids/orchid-care-sheets/oncidium/.

Snakenberg, Nick. "Orchids—A Diverse Family of Plants and People." Denver Botanic Gardens (website). February 6, 2023. botanicgardens.org/blog/orchids-diverse -family-plants-and-people.

Staake, Jill. "How to Grow a Carnivorous Sundew Plant." Birds and Blooms (website). Last updated October 28, 2022. birdsandblooms.com/gardening/flower-gardening /growing-carnivorous-plants-sundews/.

Staehling, Angela. *Happy Houseplants: 30 Lovely Varieties to Brighten Up Your Home*. San Francisco: Chronicle Books, 2017.

Stamen and Stem (website). "Plant Profiles: *Sansevieria* (Snake Plant)." April 29, 2018. stamenandstemblog.com/blog/sansevieria.

Steil, Aaron. "How Do I Care for a Philodendron?" Iowa State University Extension and Outreach (website). Last updated March 19, 2024. yardandgarden.extension.iastate .edu/faq/how-do-i-care-philodendron.

Surjushe, Amar, Resham Vasani, and D.G. Saple. "Aloe Vera: A Short Review." National Library of Medicine. 2008. ncbi.nlm.nih.gov/pmc/articles/PMC2763764/.

Tilley, Nikki, and Mary Ellen Ellis. "*Syngonium* (Arrowhead Plant): Complete Care and Gardening Guide." Gardening Know How (website). Last updated February 21, 2024. gardeningknowhow.com/houseplants/arrowhead-plant/arrowhead-plant-care -arrowhead-plant-or-syngonium-podophyllum.htm.

Toscano, Kim, and Hannah Baker. "How to Get Jasmine to Bloom Indoors." Real Simple (website). Last updated April 10, 2024. realsimple.com/how-to-grow-a-jasmine-plant-indoors-7112695#toc-how-to-get-jasmine-to-bloom-indoors.

University of Waterloo: Earth Sciences (website). "Fern Fossils." Accessed September 1, 2024. uwaterloo.ca/earth-sciences-museum/resources/history-life/carboniferous
-period/pennsylvanian-sub-period/fern-fossils.

Vanzile, Jon. "How to Grow and Care for Bird's Nest Ferns." The Spruce (website). Last updated February 25, 2024. thespruce.com/grow-asplenium-nidus-ferns-1902716.

———. "How to Grow and Care for Chinese Evergreen (*Aglaonema*) Indoors." The Spruce (website). Last updated August 5, 2024. thespruce.com/grow-aglaonema
-houseplants-1902734.

———. "How to Grow and Care for Croton Plants." The Spruce. Last updated July 18, 2024. thespruce.com/grow-codiaeum-variegatum-1902750.

———. "How to Grow and Care for Gardenia." The Spruce (website). Last updated August 20, 2024. thespruce.com/grow-gardenia-indoors-1902758.

———. "How to Grow and Care for Gasteria." The Spruce (website). Last updated January 16, 2024. thespruce.com/grow-gasteria-succulents-indoors-1902979.

———. "How to Grow and Care for Majesty Palm." The Spruce (website). Last updated August 12, 2024. thespruce.com/grow-ravenea-majesty-palms
-indoors-1902882.

———. "How to Grow and Care for Parlor Palm." The Spruce (website). Last updated January 17, 2024. thespruce.com/grow-chamaedorea-indoors-1902884.

———. "How to Grow and Care for Rabbit's Foot Fern." The Spruce (website). Last updated April 18, 2024. thespruce.com/grow-davallia-species-indoors-1902720.

———. "How to Grow and Care for Rubber Plant Indoors." The Spruce (website). Last updated August 8, 2024. thespruce.com/grow-rubber-plant-ficus
-indoors-1902755.

———. "How to Grow and Care for *Schefflera* (Umbrella Plant)." The Spruce (website). Last updated August 27, 2024. thespruce.com/grow-schefflera-plants
-inside-1902771.

———. "How to Grow and Care for String of Pearls Plant." The Spruce (website). Last updated August 2, 2024. thespruce.com/grow-string-of-pearls-succulents-1902522.

———. "How to Grow and Care for Weeping Fig." The Spruce (website). Last updated April 14, 2024. thespruce.com/grow-weeping-fig-indoors-1902440.

———. "How to Grow and Care for Zebra Plant." The Spruce (website). Last updated March 29, 2024. thespruce.com/grow-zebra-plants-inside-1902777.

Acknowledgements

From Janet and Sheryl: A huge thank you to our massively supportive, talented, and dedicated team at TouchWood Editions: Tori Elliott (publisher), Nara Monteiro (editorial coordinator), Curtis Samuel (publicist and social media coordinator), Paula Marchese (copy editor), Meg Yamamoto (proofreader), and Pat Touchie (owner). Thank you to Kate Kennedy for working with us during the initial stages of the manuscript. A very special thank you goes out to Sydney Barnes (interior design) and Tree Abraham for the stunning book covers and captivating illustrations which make us giddy with happiness!

From Janet: To all the indoor plants I have known, I thank you for all that you give to me. I do hope you enjoy being in my home.

To Sheryl, once again, my profound thanks for being my co-author as we continue this journey. Your vision, inspiration, and plain hard work as we put this book together blew my mind out the door!

May my long-suffering family continue to accept with grace and resignation the ever-increasing amount of space taken up by plant friends.

From Sheryl: This one's for my husband, Rob, who is now very familiar with the refrain "But it won't grow *too* big" every time I bring home a new houseplant. He knows I'm lying, but he sweetly grins and bears it, with only the slightest bit of eye rolling.

To my mum (who can propagate and grow pretty much any plant handed to her), my dad, and my brother Derek (who received Mum's green thumb in the genetic lottery): Thank you for everything! I love you all so much.

And to Janet: This was a bit of a departure from our usual projects, but boy, was it fun! Thank you for your continued friendship, and your dedication to our bookish projects and all the things that go along with them!

© *Steve Melrose*

About the Authors

SHERYL NORMANDEAU was born and raised in the Peace Country region of northern Alberta and has made Calgary her home since 1994. A writer and master gardener, Sheryl holds a bachelor's degree in English, as well as a Prairie Horticulture Certificate and an Urban Sustainable Agriculture Certificate. Between 2013 and 2023, she served as the online Ask an Expert for the Calgary Horticultural Society. She works at the Calgary Public Library—besides gardening, books of all kinds are her grand passion! She is a small-space gardener (on a tiny balcony and in a plot in a nearby community garden), and she is most enthusiastic about growing veggies. She lives with her husband, Rob, and their rescue cat, Smudge. Find Sheryl at Flowery Prose (floweryprose.com) and on Facebook (@FloweryProse1), X (@Flowery_Prose), and Instagram (flowery_prose).

JANET MELROSE was born in Trinidad, West Indies, and immigrated to Canada in 1964. She has lived in Calgary since 1969. She is a master gardener and the creator and owner of the successful horticulture business Calgary's Cottage Gardener, which specializes in garden education and consultation, horticultural therapy, and advocating for sustainable local food systems. She holds bachelor's degrees in sociology and history, a Prairie Horticulture Certificate, and a Horticultural Therapy Certificate. Janet is a lifelong gardener, coming from a heritage of English gardening. She has a large garden at home in the suburbs of Calgary that can only be described as a typical cottage garden. She cares for many other gardens throughout Calgary through her work as a horticultural therapist, as well as a bed at the Inglewood Community Garden. She is married to Steve and has two children, Jennifer and David. Three cats, Patrick, Theo, and Mia, currently own their home and patrol against the deer, hares, squirrels, skunk, mice, insects, and assorted birds that believe the garden is theirs, too! Connect with Janet on Facebook (@Calgarys-Cottage-Gardener), X (@CalCottageGrdnr), and Instagram (CalgarysCottageGardener).

Books by Janet Melrose and Sheryl Normandeau

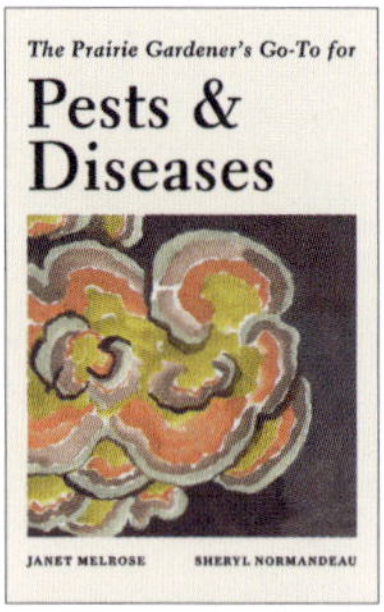